Sports Illustrated
SKIING

THE SPORTS ILLUSTRATED LIBRARY

Sports Illustrated
SKIING

by TIM PETRICK

Photography by Heinz Kluetmeier

PERENNIAL LIBRARY

Harper & Row, Publishers
New York, Cambridge, Philadelphia, San Francisco
London, Mexico City, São Paulo, Singapore, Sydney

The following people were a tremendous help in the writing of this book:
Horst Abraham, Kathe Dillmann, Chuck Goldner, Mike Porter; PSIA Demonstration
Team and Coaches Leroy Schultz, Robin Smith, Juris Vagners; and, especially, my
parents, who bought my first pair of skis, and my wife, Michelle, who is one of the best
ski teachers I know.

Special thanks to the Aspen Skiing Company, Aspen, Colorado, and the Mt. Mansfield
Company, Stowe, Vermont, for their assistance with on-snow photography, and to
Front Four Sports, Stowe, Vermont, for help with equipment.

FIRST EDITION

Library of Congress Cataloging in Publication Data

Petrick, Tim.
  Sports illustrated skiing.

  1. Skis and skiing. I. Title.
GV854.P425   1985   796.93   85-42583
ISBN 0-06-015414-4   86 87 88 89 MVP 10 9 8 7 6 5 4 3 2
ISBN 0-06-096010-8 (pbk.)   85 86 87 88 89 MVP 10 9 8 7 6 5 4 3 2 1

Contents

Sports Illustrated
SKIING

Preface

The ski bug bit me at age seven, when one wintry day my dad took me to a golf course near our home in Suffern, New York, and said he was going to teach me skiing. My boots were made of rubber, my skis were wood without metal edges, and the "lesson" involved sending me off from the top of the hill and seeing how far I could get before crashing. I'd go straight down for a ways in a wide snowplow—and inevitably lose control of the skis and fall down. Climbing back up the hill, I must have wondered why Dad was doing this to me. But as the day progressed, I kept going farther and farther before I'd crash, and, by the end of the day, the sensation of sliding on snow had me hooked.

The following year we moved to Minnesota, and I began skiing in earnest. My parents enrolled me in a year-long lesson program, and I thought I'd never learn to ski parallel. I could snowplow down anything, but no matter how many times the well-meaning man with the Austrian accent would yell at me, I could not, to my frustration, turn both skis at once—my inside leg always turned after the outside one. By the end of the winter, my edgeless skies were worn round on the insides from perpetually snowplowing, and, as much as I liked being outdoors and sliding on snow, there seemed no way to get better.

9

Twenty-plus years since the ski bug first bit him, the author loves skiing more than ever.

Then one day during my second full winter on skis, my legs started turning together. In retrospect, I realize that my ankles had started to flex more and my weight was better centered on the skis, but as a young boy I thought it was a miracle. My prayers had been answered; the door to parallel skiing was opened. The bug bit even more deep.

As the years progressed, our family skied with a certain fanaticism. We moved to western New York when I was 10 and skied every weekend and at least two nights each week. By now, my mother was resigned to being a ski widow—she couldn't ski because of serious back problems—and brother Tom and I were becoming fairly accomplished skiers. Three or four times each winter the family would pack up and drive to Vermont. Our travels took us to all of the major, and many of the not so major, areas in the state. Skiing had become a way of life.

Through all those years, and to the present, my love for skiing has only gotten deeper. I can't seem to ski enough. I taught skiing—and now coach racing—to share this love with others. I have always wanted to improve my skiing and learn better ways to convey information to my students. Through the years many great teachers have helped me in this pursuit. Robin Smith, Cal Cantrell, Stu Campbell, Horst Abraham, Chris Ryman, Jens Husted, Jerry Warren, and Mike Porter—each of them, and many others, has helped me along the way.

The purpose of this book is to share with you some of what I've learned. The first two chapters are designed as background information for the beginning skier. Chapter One gives you basic information on how to get started learning to ski. Chapter Two discusses equipment, with special emphasis on buying versus renting, and selecting the proper clothing. Chapters Three through Six are applicable to all levels of skier, and Chapter Seven provides valuable information on dryland conditioning and off-season training. As you'll see, the book has been written in ascending levels of skill acquisition, so it's best to start at the beginning to grasp the entire picture. If you don't have the time for this approach, then by all means turn to the pages that most apply to you. I have tried to include many "tips" in this book, some of which will be familiar to ski veterans. If you fall into this category, please excuse the basic nature of the opening chapters.

For those who've never skied before, I hope this book encourages you to get started. More than 15 million people are regular skiers in the United States alone. My goal with this book is to make you curious enough to find out why.

More than 15 million Americans call themselves regular skiers.

1

Getting Started

Someone might legitimately ask, "Why should I learn to ski?" After all, there are so many other forms of winter recreation. Indoor tennis or other racquet sports, bowling, snowmobiling, or even a trip to the tropics—all compete for your recreation dollars. You can sit around when it's cold outside, watch TV or read a book. Any one of these things is fun, but nothing compares with skiing. Although I'm admittedly biased, skiing is simply the best.

I say that because skiing is fun at all levels. Where most other sports require countless hours of practice to achieve even moderate success, if you are in average physical condition, have proper equipment, and receive good instruction, you can learn the basics of skiing in two hours. Surprising? Yes, but after a typical two-hour beginner ski class, almost all of the students can make simple stops and turns. True, it may take several years and many miles to become an expert skier, but the basics you learn in your first lesson are applied all along the way. There's a certain building-block quality to ski technique that makes learning really easy.

Making the decision to become a skier opens up one of the great recreational activities available

13

Easy to learn at any age, skiing is a lifelong sport.

14 today. Most obvious is the pleasure of it—the elation and freedom you experience sliding down snow-covered slopes. Cutting tracks in virgin powder snow on blue-sky days contrasts excitingly with skiing in the strange quiet of a heavy snowstorm. Regardless of the conditions, skiing is the challenge of you against the mountain, and there is tremendous satisfaction in learning to find harmony with the natural elements.

Skiing is also great exercise, and the feeling you have after being outdoors in clean air all day is superb. Sharing it with a friend—an old one, or a new one whom you met through the sport—makes it even more special. All skiers share a camaraderie based on a common enjoyment of winter in the mountains. Each individual experiences the pleasure of skiing in a unique way, but there exists a common bond among us all.

Another reason skiing is so popular is the life-long, family nature of the sport. Children can learn when they're barely old enough to walk, and there's no upper age limit for getting started. I have taught skiing to people who were in their sixties and who possessed no special athletic gifts, yet who could keep on doing it as long as they were healthy enough to walk. Of course, late starters don't go on to race in the World Cup, but they can become very proficient. Young and old can enjoy the experience together and find similar satisfaction. Skiing is a versatile recreational activity.

Skiing can literally make you feel on top of the world.

Skiing is a great family activity, and skiers share a special cama-raderie.

Getting started in the sport is a simple process. Just reading this book will give you all the background information necessary to begin. Thereafter, ski magazines like *Powder, Ski,* and *Skiing,* as well as numerous books on the sport, are references you should investigate. The more you read about skiing, the broader your understanding of the sport will be. The end result will be faster progress and fewer pitfalls toward your goal of becoming an accomplished skier.

In addition to reading about the sport, you can learn a great deal about skiing by talking about it. Each fall "ski shows" throughout the country assemble expert representatives from ski areas and equipment manufacturers from around the world. Admission charges are usually reasonable, and attending a ski show is an excellent way to talk with some of the most knowledgeable people in the industry. From ski area representatives, for example, you can hear and compare prices of learn-to-ski packages and, although you can't normally purchase equipment at these expositions, factory representatives will tell you what's new in equipment and help direct you toward skis, boots, poles, and clothing that are appropriate for your ability.

Once you get started skiing, ski shops are where you'll eventually purchase the necessary equipment. Be prepared to do some comparative shopping. Usually shops in metropolitan areas are less expensive than those right at the ski slopes. All stores have sales in late winter and spring, and if you can wait, you'll find the best deals then. Regardless of when you decide to buy, though, it's important to get some background knowledge before you venture into a shop. To repeat, written material and ski shows are your best sources of information, and you can also gain a great deal of information by talking to knowledgeable skiers. In Chapter Two, I'll tell you what you need to know about equipment so that your shopping experience is a positive one and you get what you actually need.

Price in skiing is an often discussed topic. You may be one of many who thinks that skiing is a prohibitively expensive form of recreation. Not so. Sure, you'll need to purchase a certain amount of equipment if you're going to continue as a skier, but starting out, it is possible to learn to ski rather inexpensively, as I'll show you in a moment.

As for ticket costs, an average lift ticket allows a day's worth of skiing at a rate of only $3 to $4 an hour, and you can reduce that and other ski-related costs by joining a ski club. Clubs offer fellowship, as well as reduced prices. Their buying power often allows them to organize week-long package trips to major destination resorts for $250 or less, and most packages include lifts, lodging, transportation, and, in some cases, meals and lessons.

Be warned, however, that ski clubs come in many shapes and sizes. They range from those with a strictly family orientation to those directed toward young singles. Obviously the atmosphere at club meetings and during ski trips can vary greatly. You can find out more about the different clubs in your area by consulting in the Yellow Pages and phoning the clubs for information, or by meeting members at ski shows, where clubs often solicit new members.

WHY TAKE LESSONS?

Skiing is easy, but many people learn the hard way. The typical scenario goes something like this: You have a skiing friend who insists that you should try it, and who offers to let you use his old boots (two sizes too big), an extra pair of skis (210 cm. long), and who says assuredly, "I'll teach you." You accept your friend's generosity and set a date for your first day on skis. Now you're in trouble.

The chosen day rolls around, and you set off for the slopes. Upon arrival at the ski area, you go into the base lodge to get ready. The boots seem a little big, but your friend suggests wearing three pairs of socks. You do as instructed, and the boots now grip your feet like a vise. "No problem," says the friend. "In a while they'll feel like bedroom slippers." As you head out to buy your lift ticket, you notice several ski school classes taking place on a very gradual slope off to one side. When you ask your friend if that might be a good place for you to start, he replies, "No way. That's for sissies. You'll learn a lot quicker if we go right to the top of the mountain." You have some second thoughts, but, after all, your friend must know what he's talking about.

Getting on the chair lift is an experience. You are nearly thrown to the ground at the loading area but somehow manage to stay on. As the lift moves you toward the top of the mountain, a fine layer of perspiration forms on your body. Your breathing shortens. Committed at this point, you try to remember how easy your friend told you this sport was. After an awkward fall trying to get off the chair at the top of the mountain, you follow your friend to an intermediate slope he has chosen for your initiation into the sport. On it, you spend most of the time out of balance, and take several scarifying crashes. You feel like you're standing on two banana peels on a freshly waxed floor. Each time you regain your balance and can remain stationary for a moment, your friend gives you helpful advice like, "Just keep your feet together and do it like this." After more than an hour of cursing and crashing, you make it to the

Learning to ski is easy, but many people learn the hard way.

bottom of the mountain. "Go ahead up for another run," you tell your friend, conceding defeat. "I'm going to the bar for a drink."

The scenario is fiction, but not fantasy. It has been reenacted hundreds of times over the years, and I still wonder why more people aren't hurt learning this way. A testimony to the resiliency of the human body, I suppose. Regardless, it is absolutely *crazy* to learn to ski like this! The drawbacks are just too great. One of the biggest is damaging your body. Skiing in boots that are too big, with skis that are too long, is asking for trouble. Besides the poor odds of your bindings releasing in a bad fall, as a beginner you are sure to find it nigh impossible to control full-length skis. And, beyond personal risk, you stand the very real chance of hurting other people on the slopes. Take special note of item number two in the Skier's Responsibility Code: *If you run into another skier, you are responsible,* just as though you were driving a car and ran a stoplight.

There are elements of risk in skiing that common sense and personal awareness can help reduce.

1) Ski under control and in such a manner that you can stop and avoid other skiers or objects.
2) When skiing downhill or overtaking another skier, you must avoid the skier below you.
3) You must not stop where you obstruct a trail or are not visible from above.
4) When entering a trail or starting downhill, look uphill and yield to other skiers.
5) All skiers shall wear retention straps or other devices to help prevent runaway skis.
6) You shall keep off closed trails and posted areas and observe all posted signs.

After the potential legal risks of "learning from a friend," the next main drawback is learning bad habits. Movement patterns develop when our bodies learn to fire muscles in certain sequences. If the order and timing of these movements is incorrect, your muscles, in effect, become mis-programmed. Improper turning techniques will work some of the time, but ultimately they will limit your progress and relearning the correct movements will be difficult and frustrating.

Beyond personal liability and bad habits, your experience with a home-grown approach might make you think that skiing is too hard to learn—feeling that you're just not good enough an athlete to become a skier. With this attitude you'll never experience the pleasures and joys of skiing.

No matter what a friend tells you, *the best way to learn to ski is by taking a "beginner package" at a ski area.* It will provide you with boots that fit, skis of the proper length, and bindings that are adjusted for your height, weight, and ability. In addition, you'll receive a lift ticket and a lesson of two or four hours from a professional ski teacher. The price for this package is usually $30 or less. Special deals, such as the More People on Skis Program sponsored by the Ski Industries of America, offer the beginners package for $10. More than 14,000 people registered for MPOS in 1984.

Class or group lessons are the best bet for starting out. Individual lessons are more appropriate for advanced skiers who need to work out specific problems in their skiing. Group lessons are cheaper, and the other learners in the class perform two important functions. First, they'll exhibit examples of correct and incorrect ways of doing things, and these images provide important short-cuts in the learning process. Second, class lessons are a great way to meet people. The shared experience of a group of beginners is the basis for moral support during the class and the foundation for future friendships.

Group lessons are the best way to get a successful, safe introduction to the sport.

As with other sports, the instructors are not all of equal quality. There are tremendously talented instructors who have a knack for making learning fun and communicating with their students, and there are those at the opposite end of the spectrum. After you've had a ski class, you won't need any "expert" to tell you whether or not it was a good one. You'll know. Although it is no guarantee of getting a superb class, you have a much better chance if the teacher is certified by the Professional Ski Instructors of America.

Certification of Ski Teachers in the United States

Formed in 1961, the Professional Ski Instructors of America was an organization divided into nine geographic divisions, covering all the states except Hawaii. The levels of certification in PSIA are broken down as follows:

- *Registered status* is the entry level of the PSIA. To become registered, the teacher must be a member in good standing of a bona fide ski school and attend a clinic presented by his or her geographic division.
- *Associate:* Instructors in this category are qualified to teach any skier up to the level of beginning parallel.
- *Certified:* the highest level within PSIA. Teachers with this pin have been judged to have a deep understanding of the sport and are qualified to teach all levels of ability through beginning racing.

To maintain certification, an instructor must attend a refresher clinic at least once every two years. There are currently 17,000 registered, associate, or certified instructors who belong to PSIA.

When you take a lesson, you should expect your teacher to be a member of PSIA. Instructors who belong have made a commitment to being profession-

Certified ski teachers have made a commitment to professional excellence and regularly attend refresher clinics to stay current on developments in technique and teaching styles.

als. To pass certification exams, they must be good skiers familiar with the tools necessary to teach skiing. Certified instructors also have a basic education in the related subjects of:

1) kinesiology (the study of how the human body moves)
2) basic physics (the forces produced as we slide down mountains and make turns)
3) learning theory (how people acquire motor skills)
4) teaching styles (ways of conveying information to different learners)

By understanding these subjects, a teacher can be much more effective. As you head out for your first lesson, you should realize, as we'll see next, that ski instruction has come a long ways from the days of "Bend ze knees, five dollars please."

THE EVOLUTION OF SKI INSTRUCTION

Twenty or thirty years ago in Europe, each country was trying to establish a "national technique." Austria, France, Switzerland, and Italy, as well as any other place that had snow-covered mountains, had different approaches to skiing. The reasoning behind the search for a national identity in ski technique was simple: tourist dollars. If the travelers of the world believed that a given country was "the" place to learn to ski better, they would go there on vacation. Government tourist bureaus infused large amounts of money into instructor organizations within these countries to help them define and implement their own national technique. Large schools for the study of skiing, such as the Bundesportheim in St. Christoph, Austria, became centers for research about the sport.

When PSIA was formed in the early '60s, their approach to skiing was essentially borrowed from the work of the Austrians. It included rigid techniques based on 11 "finished technical forms," and students of this linear ski methodology had to be able to perform one maneuver before moving on to the next class. Skiing, in those days, was very black and white. Instructors talked in terms of "positions" and drilled their students in very exacting forms that described the "proper" snowplow, stem christie, or parallel turn.

The problem with our American technique—and the other national approaches during this period—was that it was *too specific*. Each country tried to take one movement a skier might make in executing a given turn and build an entire technique around it. For example, the French were known for their rotation, while the Austrians emphasized counter-rotation. This made it easy to recognize a skier who was the product of a given national technique. It wasn't that the movements these techniques promoted were wrong, it's just that *no single method of turning is the foundation for a ski technique.* If it is, the technique won't be adaptable to the various situations a skier confronts on a ski slope.

The limitations inherent in a national-technique approach to skiing have been internationally recognized—a fact that was readily apparent at the last Interski, held in Sesto, Italy, in 1983. Interski is the quadrennial meeting of the world's ski instructors. Its purpose is to provide a forum where national instructor organizations like PSIA can share their ideas on teaching skiing. Each nation sends a demonstration team comprised of that country's best skiing teachers to show its approach to skiing. During the national technique era, great differences were shown on the hill. In fact, national instructor associations were "expected" to unveil new techniques, and the "winner" country could expect to realize added tourist dollars as skiers flocked there to learn the "new" way to ski.

But anyone who attended the Interski in 1983 knew that the national-technique approach was dead. To become an expert skier or simply to be adaptable to varying ski conditions, a skier has to use many different movement patterns. It has been found—and agreed upon—that there is a universal technique of function and a skier will look a certain way depending on the task at hand. No longer do instructors try to impose form on the situation; instead they now encourage the situation to dictate the form. The emphasis at the last Interski was on finding better methodologies—in short, on understanding how people learn.

The PSIA approach to ski teaching is called the American Teaching Method (ATM). ATM was first outlined in 1972 and was the product of research headed by Horst Abraham, the former educational chairman of PSIA. ATM analyzes skiing in terms of three primary skill areas: 1) *edging,* 2) *rotary,* and 3) *pressure control.* This is known as the *skills approach.* Within these broad areas can be fitted all the various movements skiers use to make turns. The skills approach has tremendous utility for the instructor. It provides an analytical tool with which to look at a student's performance and makes possible more accurate decisions concerning lesson content. The teacher knows that if he works on a given skill area, the student will have greater overall dexterity on skis. This is a tremendous improvement over years past when an instructor taught someone a stem christie because the skier signed up for a certain-level lesson.

The Universal Technique

How a person looks on skis depends on terrain, speed, turn radius, and the task at hand.

The goal of the skills approach is to produce functional, self-sufficient skiers. Unencumbered by trying to duplicate a specified form, they make movements in response to the situation at hand. By heightening the skiers' awareness of the movements required to make turns—edging, rotary, and pressure control—the approach gives them all the tools they need to deal with the realities of the ski slope.

Beyond being a change in the way we look at the mechanics of skiing, ATM has changed the way instructors teach in this country. Technique in the days prior to ATM was taught in an authoritarian, command style manner: "Do this." This sort of drill-sergeant method certainly works in many cases, but it is only one approach and is totally teacher-centered. It can produce students who are "teacher-dependent," since the teacher is the only one who can show them what to do.

The instructor of today utilizes other teaching styles in addition to the command method. As you'll discover when you take a lesson, teachers use "tasks" to shape performance and develop skills. Reciprocal teaching styles involve other members of the class as observers of their peers' techniques. Provided the teacher has communicated effectively about what to look for, class members themselves can often provide simple, effective feedback to the learner. Task and reciprocal teaching styles help shift the focus from the teacher and make the students that much more self-sufficient.

The evolution of ski instruction in the United States has definitely made learning to ski much easier. We have gone from an era where skiers are taught maneuvers to a period now where students learn the skills necessary to get down the mountain. We have said goodbye to the authoritarian drill sergeant who had only one way to teach skiing. Today's instructor is an educator specializing in motor-skill development. Besides producing versatile skiers more effectively, this approach is much more fun. No doubt as we all better understand how people learn, this progress is sure to continue.

2

Equipment

In most things you get what you pay for, and skiing is no exception. But the most expensive, top-of-the-line equipment isn't necessary when you're starting out. In fact, it's undesirable. For that matter, you should avoid buying ultra-beginners' equipment as a novice since, if you stick with skiing, you'll quickly outgrow it as you progress. I recommend that adult beginners rent equipment for their first few times on skis and *buy only when they feel they can handle skis that are "Head High" or longer.* Once you are comfortable on skis that length and feel ready to buy, the question is, how do you determine what equipment you need, and how do you purchase it with the smallest dollar outlay? This chapter will give you the background information necessary to make informed decisions.

SKIS

Skis allow you to slide on snow and obviously are a basic part of your equipment. They come in various lengths (measured in centimeters) and are produced by countless companies around the world. Major U.S. manufacturers are K2 and

27

Skis, boots, poles, bindings, and a sensible selection of ski clothes are all you need for fun on the slopes.

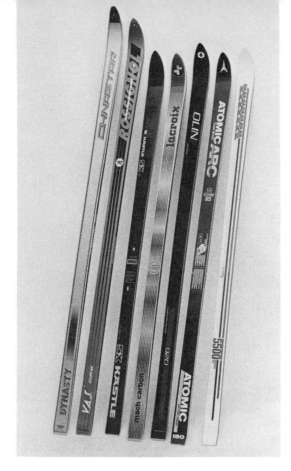

Skis come in a wide variety of models and materials, each with different characteristics. The wisest way to purchase a pair of skis is to take them out and try them on the slopes first.

Olin, although many smaller companies, such as Hexcel, Pre, and Pure Gold, also produce skis in this country.

Skis are available in two basic types: recreational or racing. Numerous marketing words, such as "sport," "compact," "high performance," and "mid series," try to define these categories further, but the general terms of recreational or racing will suffice for our discussion.

Skis of the recreational category are designed for all different levels of skier, and there are separate models for beginners, intermediates, and experts. Skis within this category are also designed for specific uses, such as cruising skis (made for making long turns at higher speeds), bump skis (which work best in the consolidated piles of snow which form on ski slopes, called moguls), and powder skis (for skiing deep snow), while all-around skis are meant to be versatile enough for all conditions. As the term suggests, all recreational skis are oriented toward skiing for fun.

Although racers also have fun skiing, their skis are engineered for more specific purposes. *Downhill skis* are designed for stability at high speeds (sometimes in excess of 70 miles per hour) and for making longer turns. *Slalom skis* are just the opposite. They are engineered for quick turns at slower speeds (around 25 miles per hour). *Giant Slalom Skis* fall somewhere in between. They are designed to make medium-radius turns and are by far the most difficult racing skis to build, since they need some of the stability of a downhill ski but must still have the flexibility to make quick turns.

If you are a recreational skier, use skis designed for general purposes. Avoid racing skis—you don't need them, and they require too much work to turn. You'll find this is true even as you become quite proficient and begin to ski in citizens' races. Recreational skis will do the job and will make the sort of skiing you usually do more enjoyable.

Design Similarities

Racing skis and recreational skis each have several things in common. The *tip* is the upcurved portion at the front of the ski, and the amount of curve the tip has is called its *splay,* which is not uniform among different skis. Generally, skis that are designed for high-speed stability (such as downhill or giant slalom skis) have a flatter curve in the tip (less splay), and skis that are designed to turn easily (slalom and recreational skis) have a steeper curve (more splay). When you are looking down on the ski, *the tip will always be the widest part.* The narrowest part of any ski, approximately at its midpoint, is called the *waist,* and this is the area where the bindings are mounted. The back of the ski is called the *tail,* which is the widest part of the ski after the tip.

If you lay a ski on a flat surface, you'll notice it only makes contact at the tip and tail—the waist is suspended in the air. This curvature is called the ski's *camber,* and there are two related reasons why the ski has it. First, it helps distribute your weight along the running surface of the ski—without it, all your weight would be carried immediately beneath your feet. Second, it makes the ski easier to turn by helping push the tip and tail into the snow when the ski is tipped on edge.

A ski's *sidecut* is determined by the dimensions of tip, waist, and tail. The combination of these parts of the ski form a barely noticeable hourglass outline when you look down on it.

Generally, skis that have more sidecut are better able to make shorter turns, and skis with less sidecut are better able to make longer ones. The impact of sidecut on the way you make turns will be discussed in Chapter Three.

If we look at a ski from the side, we see its *profile.* Every ski is thicker in the binding area and becomes gradually thinner toward the tip and the tail. Profile varies greatly among different manufacturers. Generally, metal skis have

Anatomy of a Ski

OVERHEAD

Tail (second widest)   Waist (narrowest portion)   Tip (widest portion)

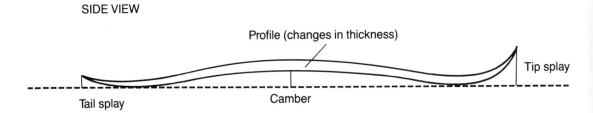

Side cut (i.e., hourglass shape)

SIDE VIEW

Profile (changes in thickness)

Tip splay

Tail splay   Camber

Testing for longitudinal flex (left) and torsional flex (right) are two ways to help determine a ski's turning characteristics.

a thinner profile and fiberglass skis are thicker. Skis with a thinner profile might seem more precise, but in practice *profile has little direct impact on ski performance.* Differences in profile are a function of the materials the manufacturer has chosen to use.

Skis also have differing degrees of stiffness, or *flex. Longitudinal flex* refers to the ski's resistance to bending along its length. A ski's stiffness can be felt by securing the tail of the ski on the floor, grasping the tip, and pushing inward at the waist. *Torsional flex* refers to the ski's resistance to twisting along its longitudinal axis. Generally, skis that are softer in torsion and flex are easier to turn, and skis that are stiffer are harder to turn. For the manufacturer, the difficulty is in blending materials so they accommodate the goals of different skiers.

Design Differences

Although the components of design discussed above are found in every ski, each company puts together the available materials in a unique way, and the materials they choose produce the characteristic "feel" of each product. Let's take a look at the various materials that make skis feel the way they do.

Core Materials

The core is the center of the ski. When a ski is being made, everything is built around the core. For this reason, its main purpose is as filler material, although it does play a minor role in overall strength. As you might expect, designers have tried many materials for use as cores.

Originally, all skis were made entirely of wood. There was no core per se, as the ski was carved from a solid piece of hickory or ash. Wood is still popular as a core material; wood cores are now made by laminating various types of wood together, then planing the lamination to the desired shape. Wood-core skis are generally thought to be *damper* (that is, less prone to vibration) and smoother on the snow than skis with other cores. From a design standpoint, the only drawbacks to wood as a core material are that it is sometimes difficult to acquire woods of consistent quality and wood is usually more expensive.

Foam is another popular core material chosen by many manufacturers because its quality is consistent and it is inexpensive to produce. Polyurethane foam, the most commonly used, is either shaped or molded to size, and skis containing such cores are usually very lively and may be somewhat lighter than their wood counterparts.

Another core material known for its lightness is aluminum honeycomb. This material, which has come to skiing from aircraft technology, has been utilized in the designs of various manufacturers over the years. Although more expensive, skis with honeycomb cores are some of the strongest on the market, and because of their extreme lightness, they have an even more lively feel than foam-core skis.

Strengthening Materials

Moving outwards from a ski's core, the next materials applied by designers both for strength and vibration-dampening purposes are the *strengthening materials,* which are applied in one of two ways:

1) Layers of fiberglass, carbon fibers, or metal are bonded to the top and bottom of the core in sheets to produce skis called *laminates,* or *sandwich construction skis* (so-called "metal" skis are actually comprised of thin layers of aluminum and, sometimes, fiberglass, sandwiching a given core material that extends all the way to the skis' sidewalls; thus, metal skis are always laminates).

2) Fiberglass or carbon fibers are wrapped around the core to produce skis of *torsion box,* or *wet wrap construction.* "Wet wrap" refers to the process of surrounding the core material with fiberglass, saturating it with resin, and baking it in a mold.

Two Basic Ski Constructions

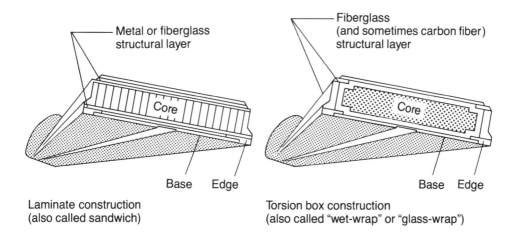

Metal or fiberglass
structural layer

Fiberglass
(and sometimes carbon fiber)
structural layer

Core

Core

Base   Edge

Base   Edge

Laminate construction
(also called sandwich)

Torsion box construction
(also called "wet-wrap" or "glass-wrap")

Beyond adding structural integrity to the ski, laminating or wrapping contributes greatly to the skis' feel—a fact that you'll discover for yourself as you start to try out skis of each construction.

Base Materials

The running surface of the ski is called the base and its purpose is to allow the ski to slide easily on the snow. Most skis today use some form of polyethylene, which is bonded onto the ski during the manufacturing process. Polyethylene comes in many varieties and the most prominent supplier for the ski industry is the InterMontana Company, based in Switzerland. Although polyethylene has been much improved in recent years, it is still one of the weak links in the durability of skis. Since it is relatively soft, it wears faster than the edges and may be gouged or scratched by icy snow and rocks.

Edges

The manufacturer also must decide which type of metal edges to use on its skis. Most common are *continuous edges*. From a manufacturing standpoint, they are the easiest to work with, contribute to the overall strength of the ski, and are generally smoother on the snow. "Cracked" edges are the other option a manufacturer has available. These edges have minute breaks along their length, which are stamped into them when they are manufactured. Although they are less smooth on the snow, the breaks in the cracked edges help dampen vibration. For this reason, a cracked-edge ski will usually hold better on very hard snow than will a ski with a continuous edge.

Length

When considering what length skis to purchase, remember that you should rent until you can handle equipment that is "head high" or longer. Purchasing very short, beginner-type skis is foolish since your ability will quickly outstrip their performance potential. When you're ready to buy, considering the following guidelines will help you make an informed decision.

Height, weight, overall strength, and skiing ability are the main factors that influence your ski length. In general, the shorter the ski the easier it is to turn, and conversely, the longer the ski the more difficult it is to turn. But don't be misled into purchasing the shortest ski possible in the hopes of becoming an instant skier. The tradeoffs of short-ski turning ease include:

1) less "stability" (that is, the ability of the ski to glide smoothly over an undulating snow surface at higher speeds)

2) less carving power (that is, the ability of the ski to cut precisely through an arc in firmer snow conditions)

3) reduced turning accuracy (constantly having to correct the path of the skis through the turn)

By selecting skis of the proper length, you will avoid the pitfalls of "shorties." Longer skis give you a smoother, more relaxed ride down the mountain, tend to hold better on ice or hard snow conditions, and their ability to turn in a precise arc will result in less fatigue. In general, I would recommend purchasing the longest ski you are comfortable turning. Although there are height/weight/ability charts provided to ski shops by the manufacturers, the best way to determine your ski length is by trying various sizes. When you "demo" a pair of skis (more on this in the "Ski Design Summary" below), be sure to make turns of different turn radii at slow and faster speeds. If possible, you should also test the skis on smooth versus bumpy slopes, and soft versus hard-packed snow to get a complete picture of how well a given length and model works for you.

Ski Design Summary

It's easy to make broad generalizations about ski performance. The popular wisdom is that laminate skis are more stable and wrapped skis are more lively, but these statements have little to do with the real world. Changes in design parameters such as sidecut or flex pattern can produce skis made out of a certain material that won't feel as they're "supposed" to. No matter how much you know about how a pair of skis were made and what they're made of, you still have to go out and try them on snow to know how they'll feel. Most ski shops have "demo" skis that they'll let you use for a nominal charge. Use them. The money you spend trying different skis is a good investment and can often be applied to the purchase price of a new pair if you decide to buy.

Ski Tuning

Regardless of what the ski is made of, it must be "tuned" for it to work properly. (Similar to drawing the best sound from a guitar by adjusting the tension of its strings, a "tuned" ski is one that has had its base and edges shaped properly for maximum performance.) Unfortunately, many people blame themselves for poor skiing performance, when it's actually the fault of their equipment. Although manufacturing techniques are improving, new skis are seldom ready to use when they arrive at the ski shop.

The reason for this is that skis go through many different steps and are handled by many different people during the manufacturing process. Machine operators make sure that the core has been placed properly in the mold, that the proper amount of resin has been applied to the fiberglass, or that the skis are sanded correctly to smooth out the edges and bases. Naturally, inconsistencies occur in the process. Machines may also be just slightly out of adjustment. And even if all these things are spot on, the resins used in the wrapping or laminating process may not cure immediately, and a ski that was perfect when it left the factory may change on its way to the ski shop.

All skis need regular tuning. This is true of new skis as well as used ones. An expert wouldn't even think of skiing on an untuned ski, and working on skis is an accepted part of a full-time skier's life. But regardless of ability level, tuning is a big factor in your comfort on a given pair of skis.

The specific steps in tuning skis are beyond the scope of this chapter. And, like tuning an automobile, the job is best left to a person who does the work on a daily basis. Ski shops have technicians who tune skis, and there are even shops at most major ski resorts that do tunings exclusively. Wherever you choose to have the work done, tuning will generally come in two forms: *belt sanding,* or *hand tuning.* Hand tuning, is far superior. Belt sanding, while usually less expensive, produces extremely inconsistent results. You should resort to belt sanding only if your skis have sustained severe rock damage and are basically beyond repair. Very often, a ski will be worse after a belt tuning than it was before you brought it in.

Hand tuning is typically done with "mill" files. The technician's basic job is to make the skis' bases uniformly flat and to file the edges so they are of

Ski Tuning

A

B

All skis, including brand new ones, should be regularly and professionally tuned for optimum performance (A).

A good ski-tuner will bevel the edges of the skis to make them easier to turn (B, C).

C

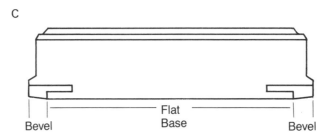

Bevel   Flat Base   Bevel

consistent sharpness along the skis' length. They will usually "bevel" the edges slightly to compensate for the tendency of the base to shrink when it is placed in the cool snow and to improve the skis' turning characteristics. Tips and tails of the skis should be dulled slightly with emery paper, and a layer of wax melted on to the bases. Ideally a pair of skis should be waxed every time you go skiing. Not only does waxing protect the bases and make the skis slide better on the snow, it also makes them easier to turn.

This is a very simplified explanation of ski tuning and is not intended to make you an expert technician. The goal is merely to alert you to the need for tuning. If you become a lifelong skier, undoubtedly you'll learn to work on skis yourself. Watching friends who are proficient in this and stroking the skis yourself are the best way to learn. Until you learn yourself, it will help to know some of the characteristics of untuned skis. By being aware of telltale signs, you can more accurately diagnose what you don't like about the way the skis are performing and communicate this information to the shop technician who'll repair them.

Performance Characteristics of Untuned Skis

Concavity in a ski means that the edges are higher than the base. If you were to hold a true bar (a piece of metal that has been machined to an exact straight edge) on the base of the ski, light would show through beneath the bar. Concave skis are very difficult to turn because their edges are literally dragging in the snow. They are also very erratic while running straight, tending instead to go off in different directions.

A *convex* ski is one where the base is higher than the edges. If you held the true bar, it would rock from side to side, since the bar only made contact in the center of the base. Convex skis feel very unstable and seem to "swim"

SKIS WITH CONCAVE AND CONVEX BASES

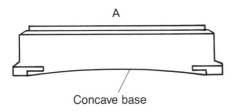

Concave base

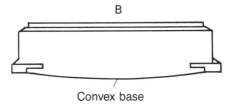

Convex base

Skis with concave bases (A) are difficult to turn.

Skis with convex bases (B) are "squirrelly"—they seem to swim all over the snow.

when you are sliding on them. Another word skiers often use to describe convex-base skis is "squirrelly."

Edge sharpness is a final problem addressed by ski tuning. If the edges are too sharp, the ski will be extremely difficult to turn and will slip sideways with a "grabby" feel. An easy way to take care of this is to run a piece of emery paper over the edges to dull them slightly. Lack of uniform edge sharpness is a more serious turning problem and is especially prevalent with new skis. Sharp and dull areas along the edges will make it impossible to turn smoothly. Skis with uneven sharpness perform as a car does if you repeatedly make small turning motions with the steering wheel as you go around a curve.

If your skis exhibit any of the above symptoms, bring them to a ski shop or a specialty ski-tuning shop for repair. Remember, ask for hand tuning, and don't believe the clerks if they say a belt will do just as good a job—even if they brag about their expensive "stone grinding" machine. Hand tuning costs more, but it is really the only way to get maximum performance from a pair of skis.

BOOTS

Boots are the most important part of your ski equipment. By supporting your feet and lower legs, they help you maintain balance and transmit turning power to the skis. Boots all have two main design components: a *shell,* the exterior part of the boot that you can see, and an *inner boot,* the part actually in contact with your foot.

Today's ski boots are much better than earlier models. As little as 20 years ago, putting on a ski boot and getting used to it was a true test of dedication. Boots then were made of specially tanned leather. Since this material was extremely stiff, your foot had to learn how to fit the boot. Full-time skiers would spend three or four weeks getting used to a pair of boots, only to have the leather wear out and fatigue a few months later. Leather boots also required tedious maintenance to protect them from quick deterioration. Special preservatives were required to keep the leather pliable and waterproof, and "boot trees" were necessary to prevent the soles from curling.

Today's ski boot is much more user-friendly. Most shells are made of some type of polyurethane, which is durable and requires virtually no maintenance. Those characteristics produce boots that have controlled flexes, so that they are comfortable yet do an excellent job of transmitting turning power to the skis.

Although many companies make ski boots, the outer shells that they manufacture fall into three basic closure types. First are the so-called *overlap*

All boots have an outer shell (left), which transmits turning power to the skis, and an inner boot (right), which surrounds the foot to provide comfort, warmth, and additional support.

boots. These have an overlapping shell that is closed by three to five buckles and are often considered to be more appropriate for advanced skiing and racing. The second main category of ski boots is *external-tongue* models. These have a lower shell, which opens over the instep, and an external tongue, which can be pushed out of the way during foot entry. Many skiers find external-tongue boots easier to get into than overlapping boots, but well-made models of either type provide excellent sensitivity to the skis. The third main category of ski boots is the *rear-entry models.* Initially boots of this type were known for good fit but low performance. Early rear-entry models tended to seriously inhibit ankle-flex and reduce a skier's sensitivity to the skis. In recent years, this problem has been eliminated and rear-entry boots are available that provide excellent performance characteristics while maintaining the comfort they were always known for. Consequently, *the decision on whether to buy one type of boot or another should be based on how comfortable a given shell design feels to you.*

The inner boots that go inside these shells are designed in a number of different ways. Most prevalent are the totally synthetic variety. Synthetics— mostly nylon blends—are easier for the manufacturer to sew together, making the boots much less expensive to produce. Some companies back the inner surfaces that touch the foot with leather or with a wool blend. Leather has a very soft feel but tends to trap moisture. Wool blends do a good job of holding the foot in place thanks to the fibrous nature of the material, and they tend to be warmer. In addition, a few manufacturers mold inner boots out of neoprene rubber. These boots tend to be quite warm, but, because of neoprene's friction characteristics, are often difficult to get on and off.

No matter what your inner boots are made of, *you must be sure to reli-*

Three Types of Ski Boots

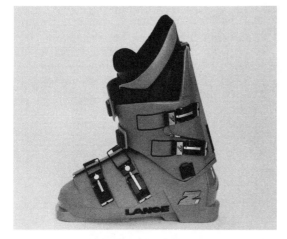

Overlapping closure

External tongue

Rear-entry

The choice of which type of boot to buy is largely a matter of comfort.

giously dry them out. However warm the manufacturer claims the boots are, if they're not bone dry when you go skiing you'll have cold feet. For best results, take the inner boots out and suspend them over a moderate heat source. Another way to ensure warm feet, experienced skiers know, is to put on clean, dry socks just before you buckle up the boots. In addition, *never* store your boots in the trunk of your car on your way to the ski hill. If you do they'll chill up like an ice box and your feet will get cold.

Deciding on which brand and model of boot to buy can be extremely confusing. Products of every shape and color are available. There are a number of things to consider when shopping for the right ski boot.

First, *plan on spending several hours at it.* You are purchasing something your feet will live in for five to eight hours at a stretch, every time you go skiing. Make sure the boots are comfortable.

Second, *go to a reputable ski shop.* If you have a friend who skis, have him recommend one. Good shops have salespeople who expect to take an hour or more to fit a pair of boots—they will not try to shove you out the door so they can get to the next customer.

Third, *make sure you have socks of similar weight to the ones you plan on skiing with.* Buying a pair of boots that fit you in lightweight dress socks will make you absolutely miserable when you put on heavier ski socks. I recommend wearing a single pair of medium-weight, wool-blend ski socks. Wearing more than one pair of socks, or one pair that's extremely thick (such as hunting socks), will eliminate your sensitivity in the boots. You want your foot as close to that inner boot as possible.

Fourth, *describe honestly what type of skier you are when the salesperson asks.* His or her decision about what model boot is appropriate depends upon your ability level. A reputable shop handles proven products and will sell you no more or less boot than you need. At the beginning levels of skiing, it is desirable to wear a softer boot. You should be able to bend your ankle in it quite easily. Softer boots are less reactive when you apply turning power to the skis. By contrast, buying a pair of competition boots as a beginner is much like getting a Porsche 928 for your first car. You might live through the experience, but the product will really make you work.

Finally, *wear the boot for at least 40 minutes in the store.* An hour is better. It takes that long for foot cramps or pressure points to develop. So many people, myself included, have left a ski shop thinking that they've just bought the most comfortable pair of boots ever, only to be disappointed on the slopes. Flex your ankles, walk around the store, check out other merchandise. You must give yourself ample time to figure out whether the boots fit.

When buying a pair of ski boots, be sure to tell the salesman what level skier you are, and plan on wearing the boots for an hour to make sure they don't cramp your feet.

By the way, don't expect a ski boot to feel like your old tennis shoes or Top Siders, but don't believe any salespeople who say all ski boots hurt and the pain will go away in time. If they tell you that, *get out of there and find a ski shop whose salespeople know what they're talking about!* A ski boot should be snug, but not uncomfortable. It should feel like someone is firmly grabbing hold of your foot (primarily the area around your ankle) with two hands. Your toes should not be touching the end of the boot, and you should be able to wiggle them freely. If you are an advanced skier, your toes may have light contact with the end of the boot but should pull away when you flex your ankles. In any case, if your feet go to sleep or get tingly, the boots won't work.

Don't despair on the first try if you can't find a pair of boots that feel quite right. The reason there are so many boot manufacturers around is that feet are like fingerprints—each one is unique to the individual. Take the time to find a pair that feels good on your feet. Too many people have given up skiing because their feet hurt, and there's no reason for this. Excellent ski boots are available today, and there are many people qualified to help you find them. I spend well over 1,000 hours each winter in my ski boots, and when they go on at eight o'clock in the morning, they usually don't come off until five that evening. You can almost live in boots that fit.

A recent development in boot comfort is the molded insole. Most of these

insoles are made from either cork or a hard plastic material that is covered with
a soft foam. Ski shops can custom fit them to your feet by heating the insoles
in a small oven, then having you stand on top of them for several minutes.
While not a corrective, orthotic device, custom insoles do fill in all the nooks
and crannies on the soles of your feet, and this total contact with the sole of
the boot results in improved control and greater comfort.

BINDINGS

Beyond the rules of common sense discussed in the "Skiers' Responsibility
Code," the most important items in ski safety are your bindings. Tremendous
improvements have been made in the design of bindings in recent years, and
there are many different brands to choose from. Since your safety depends on
the binding functioning properly, it is extremely important not to skimp when
purchasing this part of your equipment.

A binding is designed to perform two main functions: *retention* and *release.* The goal is to have a piece of hardware that holds you on the skis as you
go over the dips and doodles of the mountain, but lets go and separates you
from the skis when you get into trouble. Building something like this is extremely difficult, but, with high technology and many thousands of research
dollars, bindings manufacturers have been able to design "smart" products.
Today's ski binding differentiates between forces that you normally encounter
in skiing and forces that may injure you. When there's a threat to your body,
a binding should release smoothly and quickly.

Most bindings have two parts: a toe, and a heel. All bindings manufactured
today include a ski brake: a metal, pronglike device that prevents a ski from
sliding down the mountain when the binding releases. All toe pieces release in
the lateral planes, and many also provide for a twisting, upward release. The
sole of the ski boot must be designed with a certain shape (called a DIN
specification) that allows it to fit into the toe piece. Heel pieces provide release
in forward falls and come in two varieties: the *step-in heel piece,* and the
manually latching heel piece. Either type works well, and the choice is mainly
one of convenience. You don't have to bend over to get into a pair of step-in
bindings.

Regardless of the type you choose, your bindings must be adjusted regularly. Most companies recommend adjustments once at the beginning of the
season, then once or twice during the year. Ski or rental shops have specially
certified technicians to perform this job. As when purchasing boots, it is important for you to be honest when the technician asks you how good a skier you

Bindings

Step-in bindings are more convenient (top), but there are skiers who prefer manually latching bindings (bottom). Both, when properly set, release well.

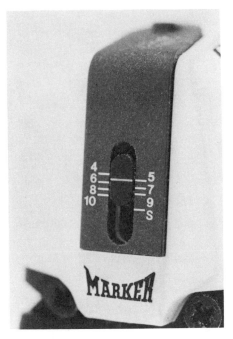

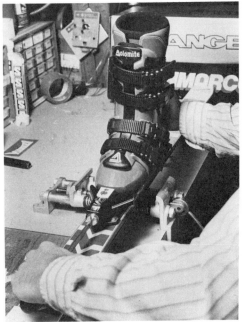

Binding settings are located on both the heel and toe pieces. The lower the setting, the more easily the binding will release during a fall.

Bindings should be professionally adjusted several times during the season.

are. Binding settings are based on ability, as well as height and weight.

Integral to the proper function of the binding is the condition of your boot soles. They generally deteriorate from walking around on hard surfaces, and this can have a negative effect on release consistency. You can prevent boot sole wear by not walking on hard surfaces—such as the parking lot at a ski area. Put your boots on in the base lodge if at all possible.

POLES

Ski poles are often an overlooked part of a skier's basic equipment. People will frequently purchase the cheapest poles possible in an attempt to cut back on the costs of skiing. This is a mistake. Cheaper poles are generally heavier and much more prone to bending or breaking. You will end up replacing them more often, and it is no fun carrying around a pair that feel like baseball bats.

All of the name-brand ski poles are very similar. With the exception of

Poles

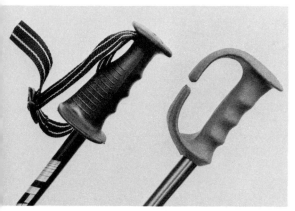

Poles with old-style strap grips (left) allow the wrists to function more naturally than those with the new saber-style grip (right).

All poles have some sort of circular basket.

exotic, expensive, and generally unnecessary carbon fiber models, they are made with the same quality aluminum. The only real difference is the "grips" the manufacturers use. Poles come with either the old-style *strap grips* or the new *saber* style. This is a case where older is better. Saber grips tend to inhibit the movement of your wrist and force you into an awkward arm movement to place your pole in the snow. They are simpler to get on and off, but the performance tradeoff is not worth it. Buy a pair of poles with the old-style grips, but make sure they have releaseable straps. This is very important should your pole basket get stuck on something.

Never ski without a basket on your pole. The basket is designed to prevent the pole from burying itself in deep snow when you plant it. If you lose a basket, take your hand out of the strap and immediately go to the ski shop to get the basket replaced. You can be seriously injured using a pole without a basket.

TO BUY OR TO RENT?

Now that we've gone through the basic equipment you need, the question is whether you should buy or rent it. The answer depends on many factors. Some people need to make a financial commitment to a sport if they're going to stay with it. Others can rent their equipment and be just as dedicated. There are also logistical considerations. If your home is far from where you'll be skiing, it might be more convenient to rent equipment than to travel with it. Whether or not you live close to a ski area, the one thing you should definitely purchase is ski boots. The sport will be much more enjoyable, and you will progress faster. Ski racers add credence to the argument for buying boots. Although a world-class skier might have up to 10 or 15 pairs of skis, he often uses just one pair of boots. Racers protect their boots with an almost weird possessiveness and use them until they're old and completely broken down. They do this because having a pair of boots that performs well eliminates a variable that could otherwise stand in the way of making their skiing more consistent.

Recreational skiers should follow the racers' example. Find a comfortable pair of boots that performs well for you, and take care of them. Always buckle them up when you put them away—even if it's just overnight. Buy new boots only when you have outgrown the performance capabilities of the model you initially purchased. When traveling by air, always carry these treasured possessions in a boot bag. These bags are available at any ski shop for a reasonable price and will fit easily under the seat in a plane. Boot bags are also convenient for carrying hats, gloves, goggles, and most anything else you'll absolutely need when you arrive at the slopes.

Owning the rest of the equipment you need to ski will also help make you more consistent. Skis have characteristic feels and begin to feel very comfortable after you've used them for a time. It's also nice to be familiar with the operation of your bindings, since rental skis come with all different brands. A rule of thumb is to *buy equipment if you ski more than one week a year.* If you ski less than this, the dollar outlay is not worth the performance sacrifice you make when you rent equipment.

Renting Equipment

There are many places to rent ski equipment. Most ski areas have their own rental facilities right at the base of the slopes. These are usually the most expensive option, unless the rental equipment is included as part of a learn-to-ski package. Other places are ski shops in the town near the ski area or in metropolitan areas. Although ski-town shops are probably the more expensive of the two, they are a much better alternative. If you rent from a store that is far from the ski area, binding adjustments will cost extra and you won't be able to make an exchange should something malfunction.

Speciality ski rental operations also exist, and these are often the least expensive. Since it is their only business, they often offer the best tuned skis and will probably have high-performance rentals for advanced skiers as well. These stores, and ski area rental facilities and ski shops offer multi-day pricing. If you are going to a ski area for several days, check into these packages to save money.

Buying Equipment

If you decide to purchase your equipment, ski shops are by far the safest route to take. You will pay a little more for the expert advice available at these stores, but you can be assured that the products you purchase will be carefully matched to your ability level. You can also be sure that the bindings will be mounted properly on the skis. Avoid discount stores and general sporting goods outfits—they just don't offer the same security.

One way to save on ski equipment is to purchase during sale periods. Ski shops usually have great bargains in the early fall and early spring. Fall sales are intended to reduce inventories and to address cash flow problems these stores might have at that time of year. Although the sale items will usually be leftover models from last year, there is nothing wrong with this equipment. In the case of skis particularly, the only difference between year-old models and new ones might be the cosmetics.

Spring sales start no later than the Presidents' Holidays. Although from a ski shop owner's point of view this is an unfortunate fact of the business, these sales allow you to purchase this year's equipment at 30 or 40 percent less than regular retail. All you have to do is wait 'til mid-February. And there are some shops, the pariahs of the industry, that have sales right after Christmas. It makes sense to watch the newspapers and to purchase ski equipment when the best bargains are available.

Another way to find bargains on equipment is to look for "ski swaps." These events are usually held by ski clubs each fall and offer supermarket-style ski shopping. Large exhibition halls or gymnasiums are rented out, and the club displays used equipment that people want to sell. Provided you know what you're looking for, this can be the least expensive way to purchase the things you need. Since all sales are final, it helps to have an experienced skiing friend with you to help distinguish the bargains from the bombs. After you have been skiing for a while, you'll find you start looking forward to your local ski swap as a way to make a few dollars by passing on equipment you are no longer using. Consignment rates vary, but the sponsoring organization usually takes about 20 percent of the asking price.

If you know what you're looking for, ski swaps are great places for finding used equipment or for selling your old boots and boards.

SKI CLOTHING

I hate being cold. My home heating bill is usually much too high, I always seem to be wearing more clothes than my friends, and I am also prone to shivering. Although surfing is one of my favorite pastimes, I turn blue in water that's anything less than tropical. Wet suits don't seem to help that much. Despite these facts, I make my living being outside in all types of winter weather for around two hundred days each year. How did a person who loves to be warm take up a sport that is purportedly so cold?

The answer is by using the right clothing. Skiing can be completely comfortable if you're wearing the right gear. Many people don't dress properly for skiing. Over the years, I've watched countless beginning skiers who came out on snowy days in jeans, a sweatshirt, and no hat. By the end of two hours their pants were soaking wet and they were nearly hypothermic. If their first experience on skis was their last, it would be no surprise. You just can't enjoy skiing if you're dressed that way.

Not dressing properly for skiing also inhibits your performance. Muscles and ligaments that aren't warm are much more susceptible to injury. Reaction times are slowed when we are cold, and this is very bad in a sport in which you must adjust to constantly changing situations. It is also harder to pay attention to your ski teacher when you're wondering whether any minute you're going to turn into an ice cube. On the other hand, it is no better to wear so many clothes that you end up perspiring. Overheating causes premature fatigue and eventually leaves you colder. Maintaining a thermostatic balance is the goal of proper dressing for skiing. It will make you feel better and improve your performance on the slopes.

Layering is the best way to dress for skiing, and the concept is very simple. Articles of clothing are combined to form various strata of insulation around the body. It begins with the layers closest to the body, which trap heat and wick away perspiration. Next come the intermediate layers. Their job is to maintain a warm layer of trapped air. Finally, the exterior garment forms a protective membrane. This keeps wind, cold air, and water (in the form of wet snow or rain) from cooling the warmth-building inner layers. The beauty of this approach to dressing is that you can add or subtract various layers to maintain the desired inner temperature.

Specifics

The first layer of protection in dressing for cold is *long underwear.* Although polypropylene "long johns" are a little more expensive than the old waffle-style hunting-type, they do a much better job of wicking off moisture caused by perspiration. *Ski socks* are also a must (see the section on boots). The final inner layer is a zip style *turtleneck.* Zip necks are nice because they allow you to "thermostat" this first layer of clothes. Ideally the turtleneck should be made of silk, wool, or polypropylene, since these are the most effective fabrics for allowing perspiration to pass through.

After these inner layers, you have a number of options depending on where you are skiing and what the weather conditions are. *Stretch pants* are appropriate for moderately cold days and are designed for flexibility and water repellency. The better pants have high percentages of wool, which makes them warmer and dryer, and many of these better pants are cut high around the back of the waist to help keep the kidneys warmer. This is extremely important. Certain models also have pads on the knees, a feature originally developed to save ski racers from bruises when they bumped into the gates. Padded pants can be a good investment for recreational skiers. The padding helps keep your knees warm and may therefore help to reduce strain on the ligaments of the knees. Unless you are very serious about racing, stay away from ski pants with hard pads. Soft ones are usually less expensive and perform the job equally well in recreational skiing.

The next layer for the torso is traditionally a *ski sweater.* Wool is the warmest, but stay away from too heavy a knit. Very thick sweaters tend to restrict movement and are too warm to be versatile in the layering process. Many skiers are now using running tops or warm-up jackets to replace a sweater. The full zipper in these garments allows for easy thermostating. Another option here is some sort of *fleece jacket.* This material, which is made from a knitted weave of polyester, provides an excellent layer of lightweight warmth and remains effective when wet. For particularly cold conditions you can wear a vest on top of your sweater, running top, or fleece coat, to add another layer of warmth.

For very cold conditions you'll also need a *ski jacket* and *warm-up pants* (also called *bib overalls*). These garments are filled with either the traditional goose down or some synthetic insulating material. Down is the number one insulator in cold, dry climates. Synthetics work best where it is usually more damp, since they don't lose their insulating power when wet. Jackets, shells, and warm-ups are usually covered by some sort of nylon blend or by a water-resistant fabric like Gore-Tex. The choice for exterior material is again determined by the type of weather conditions you usually ski in.

One weather condition many people shy away from is rain. This is unfortunate because skiing in the rain can be excellent with great snow conditions and short lift lines. Most people aren't prepared for such skiing, but a good rain suit makes it possible. Although plastic-coated products offer the best wetness protection, they don't breathe and mobility is often restricted. The Gore-Tex fabric lamination is the best material for the job. Products made with it will keep you quite dry during a rainy day on the slopes and are useful for wet snowstorms, too. These garments usually come in the form of a separate upper shell and side-zipping pants. Because of the breathability of the Gore-Tex laminate, these items are also useful as alternative outer layers when it isn't cold enough for a ski jacket or warm-up pants.

The final things you'll need for a complete set of ski clothing are *hand protection, goggles or sunglasses,* and a *hat.*

Keeping your hands warm is best done with mittens, but gloves allow you to feel the poles much better. Depending on how cold it is where you ski, I would recommend trying to use gloves if possible. For serious wet-weather skiing you'll need some rubber gloves. Buy an inexpensive pair from a hardware store, and use wool liners inside them.

A wool ski hat is essential. You can lose almost 50 percent of your body heat through your head, and not wearing a hat on cold days is an invitation to illness.

Goggles or sunglasses can help protect a portion of your face from the wind, as well as filter out the harmful rays of the sun. It is very easy to become

Clothing: How to Layer

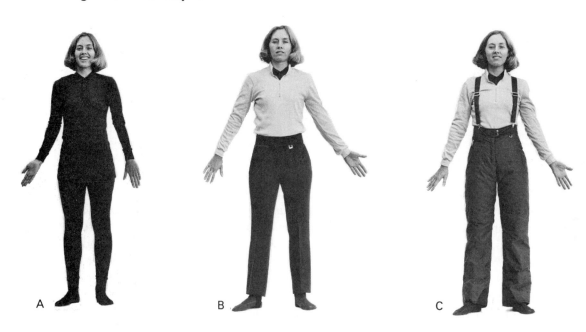

A   B   C

The best way to dress for skiing is in layers, starting with a pair of polypropylene long underwear (A), which wicks moisture and perspiration away from the body. Next, add a zip turtleneck, whose neck lets you "thermostat" the first layer, and for moderately cold days a pair of stretch pants (B). Insulated bibs (C) will keep you warm in colder weather, and a ski sweater (D) or a synthetic fleece jacket (E) forms the necessary intermediate layer. Top everything off with an insulated parka (F) or jacket (G), along with hat, boots, goggles or sunglasses, and gloves or mittens. On rainy days try a water-resistant rainsuit (H).

G   H

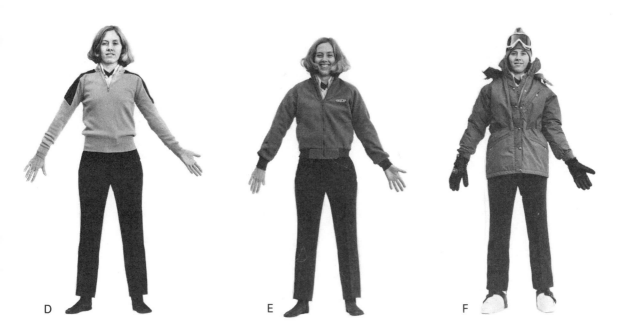

D   E   F

"snow blind" (a condition characterized by a sharp burning sensation in the eyes) when bright sun is being reflected off the snow, especially at higher altitudes. Buy goggles or glasses that are capable of filtering out ultraviolet and infrared rays from the sun.

The final layer you should be concerned about is skin that is exposed to this sunlight. Between the reflective qualities of snow and the effect of high altitude, you have the potential for severe sunburn. The first time I skied in the West I didn't really believe this and ended up with horrible (and very embarrassing) blisters all over my face. Don't make this mistake. Use high-protection-number sunscreens when you're in the mountains, and reapply them often.

Although eye and skin protection are mandatory, how you apply the rest of the preceding information is very subjective. The two main considerations are: 1) what part of the country you'll be skiing in, and 2) the capacity of your internal furnace to produce heat. Cold sensitivity is a function of how good your circulation is, and of some psychological factors. Thus, each person requires different amounts of clothing to stay warm in the same conditions. Wherever you fit on the spectrum, purchasing the right ski clothes will make the worst days tolerable, and the perfect ones even better.

3

The Fundamentals

Skiing can be a mysterious activity to an untrained observer. When standing at the bottom of a ski hill, it's hard to tell how someone manages to stay in balance while sliding down a mountainside on two narrow slats. This is even more difficult to understand in the very good skier. The expert's technique is concealed by fluidity, grace, and an utter absence of unnecessary movement. "Experts make difficult things look easy, not the other way around," Gary Berger, assistant ski school director at Mammoth Mountain, California, has said.

Regardless of the skiers' ability, the way they get down the mountain is determined by what's physically possible and how the human body can move. In more sophisticated language, technique is governed by: 1) the laws of physics, 2) equipment design, and 3) anatomy. This applies whether you're a first-day beginner or a world-class racer.

In controlling their descent down mountains, all skiers unconsciously deal with these factors. Although an exhaustive discussion of physics, equipment design, and the mechanics of human movement is beyond the scope of this chapter, there are a few things you should know to understand ski technique. For a more complete analysis

55

All skiing technique is governed by the laws of physics, by equipment design, and by human anatomy.

Like any other sport, skiing is a process of acting and reacting—there's no room for technical analysis while you're doing it.

of the elements of physics and equipment that make skiing possible, read the book *Skiing Mechanics* by John Howe (Poudre Publishing Co., 1983).

In practice, it doesn't help you to be aware of these elements while skiing. Have you ever tried to analyze the biomechanics of a golf swing while teeing off, or really considered the physics of your forehand during a tennis match? If you did, you probably made a lousy shot, or a horrible return. Technical analysis is inappropriate during performance. As with other sports, understanding what's going on might satisfy your curiosity, but you can't concern yourself with the whys and wherefores while you're doing it. Instead you simply have to act and react. With this in mind, the following information should be assimilated before you actually go out on the slopes.

The act of skiing is a very complex physical activity. By bringing you to the top of a mountain, chair lifts put you in a position where gravity can pull you back down. How fast you get pulled down the mountain is a function of how steep the slope is, your weight, how well your skis slide given the snow conditions, and the resistance of the air you are traveling through.

These factors' relative importance is determined by the conditions, with slope steepness the most obvious. Gravity makes you tend to slide faster on steeper slopes than on shallow slopes. Gravity also makes heavier people tend to go faster on a given slope. The sliding capabilities of your skis can dramatically influence how fast you'll travel down a given slope. Snow comes in many forms. It can be extremely slippery in certain conditions, or it can cling like glue to the bottoms of your skis. Moisture content (wet to dry), consistency (hard packed—bordering on ice—to powder), and the shape of the snow crystals (very old, rounded-off crystals, to sharp new ones) all influence how well your skis will slide. You can augment sliding with wax or special base preparations, but there are certain conditions that are very difficult to slide in. Extremely cold conditions (well below zero degrees Fahrenheit) or the very wet snow you often encounter in late spring is nearly impossible to get good sliding on.

Air resistance can be equally important. If you stand tall on the skis, you present more surface area to the windstream and consequently go slower. A low stance, such as the downhill racer's "egg position," allows you to go much faster down a slope, and wind direction can also have a large influence on your speed.

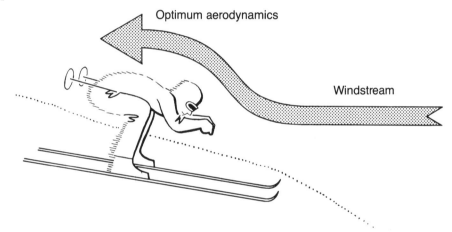

Optimum aerodynamics

Windstream

The downhill racer's "egg" position, or tuck, exposes less surface area to the windstream and results in higher speeds.

Regardless of the speed at which you are traveling, your body will take the line of least resistance down the mountain if the force of gravity is not resisted. This is called the "fall-line." It refers to the path a ball would roll along if it was released at the top of a slope. Because of the different facets of pitch that are inherent on most ski slopes, the fall-line isn't usually straight up the mountain. The fall-line varies, and an awareness of it is important in skiing. As in sanding wood, it is much easier to go with the grain than to go against it. In skiing, we want to control our speed down the slope by making turns back and forth *across* the fall-line, rather than skiing at a diagonal to it. (Although most instructors dislike the word "fall-line" because it has a negative connota-

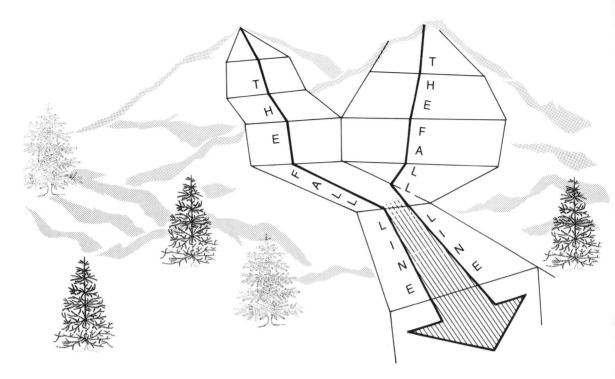

The fall-line is the line of least resistance down the mountain and varies with the mountain's different facets of pitch.

tion, no one has come up with a better term to describe this path of least resistance.)

If you were simply to allow yourself to go straight down the fall-line, the result could very well be disastrous. The solution is turning. By changing your direction right and left down the slope you control your speed. Turns happen when the edges of your skis, in concert with your weight, supply resistance against the snow. In a sense, your body is pushed around the turn as the skis are deflected by the snow.

Edge change is the most fundamental aspect of making skis turn. If you're heading across the hill on your right-hand edges, you can do anything in the world to go in the other direction, but you won't get there until you get the skis on the other edges. Edge change is accomplished in one of two ways. Either you change them sequentially by pushing the tail of your uphill ski away from you (called *stemming*) and following with the other ski, or you change both edges at once. The latter, called *simultaneous edge change,* is something of a misnomer, since both skis rarely change from one edge to the other at exactly the same moment.

Even though edge change is essential to make a turn, a turn that involved only edge change would be of little use since the radius of such a turn would be extremely long. *Rotary power* is the torque action your body produces to guide the skis through useful turns, and there are many forms of it. *Foot steering* is the most basic method and is used in wedge turns. Since the foot obviously cannot turn much without the involvement of the leg, foot steering is actually a subtle form of leg rotation. *Two-legged rotation,* similar to the mechanics of an ice skater's "hockey stop," is a more sophisticated method for producing rotary power. Rotating the legs simultaneously (which is a fancy way of saying "twisting both feet in one direction") is often described by its French name, *braquage,* which literally means "to change the direction of." There are several other methods of producing rotary power, and they will be discussed at length in subsequent chapters. For now, simply realize that to make effective turns, you need to augment ski deflection with some sort of torque action. Rotary skills are how we do this.

No matter which method you use to generate rotary power, the act of changing direction (turning) creates forces you have to deal with. Foremost of these is the same force that sends a coffee cup off the dashboard as your car turns a sharp corner. Although there is much discussion among ski technicians concerning the proper jargon to describe this, most people think of it as centrifugal force. Every time you go right or left on skis, centrifugal force tries to pull your body toward the outside of the turn. At the beginning of the turn this outward pull is very slight, but as the turn continues it gets progressively stronger.

This outward pull has two effects. First, it tries to keep you moving in a straight line rather than turning, and second, it tries to tip you over. This tipping tendency happens since centrifugal force acts through your center of mass (approximately just below your navel) but the opposing (centripetal) force acts through your skis and feet. Therefore, your feet are the fulcrum for the forces pulling you to the outside. In response, you have to move your body inside the path of the skis. How far is determined by the strength of the centrifugal force. The overall strength of this force is a function of the speed at which you are traveling and the radius of the turn you are making.

Turn radius is determined by the intensity and duration of:

1) rotary power
2) leverage
3) edge angle

The effect of rotary power should be obvious. The more torque you apply to the skis, the tighter the turn. In terms of skiing, *leverage means where you apply*

Edge Change

There are two ways to shift from one set of edges to another when skiing: sequentially, or simultaneously.

B

C

D

E

Sequential edge change

The skier initiates a turn by pushing the tail of his uphill ski away from him (A,B). This is called "stemming." He then draws the other ski parallel to the stemmed ski and turns (C,D,E). For other examples of sequential edge change, see Converging and Diverging Step Turns (pages 106 and 109).

D

C

A

B

Simultaneous edge change

Here, the skier rolls his weight from his skis' right-hand edges (A,B) to their left-hand edges (C,D) to turn the skis simultaneously from right to left.

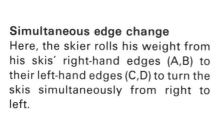

A

Rotary Power: Braquage

To make effective turns, you must augment edge change with some sort of torque action, or rotary power. Here is an excellent example of two-legged rotation known as *braquage*. Note that even though the skier's lower body has rotated sideways, his upper body remains facing down the hill.

A

B

C

D

pressure on the skis. Although it's not a blanket rule, levering the tip creates shorter-radius turns, while levering the tail makes longer ones. Edge angle refers to how much the ski is tipped up on the snow. In general, the higher the edge angle, the tighter the turn radius, and the lower the edge angle, the longer the turn.

Regardless of radius, when making turns you try to direct your body's resistance to the effects of centrifugal force into the outside ski. In other words, *you try to keep your weight on the left ski when turning to the right and on the right ski when turning to the left.* Shifting your weight from one ski to another is called *weight transfer.* You can turn with your weight on the inside ski, and

Weight Transfer

A

B

C

As the skier turns left, her weight is primarily on her right-hand ski (A). To turn right, she shifts her weight to the left-hand ski (B), and she keeps it there (C) until the turn is completed.

this can be a useful exercise to develop your balance, but it is less effective for a number of reasons. First, balancing on the inside ski is more precarious, since if the ski slips you have nowhere to go but down on your hip. Second, your outside leg is much stronger than your inside leg when it comes to resisting these forces. Finally, balancing on your inside ski forces you to move your body much further to the inside to avoid being tipped over by the forces pulling you outward.

There are two main ways to balance the outward forces created by turning. One is *banking*. This means leaning your entire body into the direction of the turn. When motorcycle riders or bicyclists make turns, that is exactly what they are doing. Banking can be a relaxing way to make turns, but it is not always the ideal method. One problem is that it's easy to lean in too far and end up with your weight on the inside ski. Another is that it is difficult to make adjustments in lean angle when the entire body is involved. You can get "caught" inside the turn and be committed to a turn radius you don't want. In spite of these facts, a banked relationship with the skis can be appropriate in certain situations. At very high speeds it is the only way you can get enough of the body inside the turn to keep you from being tipped over by the tremendous outward forces.

The second method you can use to develop inward lean in turns is *angulation* which is usually preferable. As the name implies, angulation involves making angles in your body such that the knees and hips are leaned into the turn, and the upper body is leaned out of the turn. If you look at a skier who is angulating, the body forms a sort of banana shape. The banana is best in most turns, because it is much easier to make minute adjustments from this position to balance the outward forces created by turning.

However you choose to balance the effects of centrifugal force, all turns involve speeding up and slowing down. By moving toward the fall-line you accelerate, and by moving through the fall-line you decelerate. This is important to note, because many skiers have a "fall-line phobia." They don't trust the fact that even though they speed up as they start the turn, they will slow down when they finish it. Consequently, many beginning skiers will rush the beginning of the turn in an attempt to get to the secure, slowing-down phase at the end. Ski teachers call this the "windshield-wiper turn"—a turn where the skis have been twisted with too much force. You have to learn to trust yourself and your skis and know that you will regain control with the ending phase of the turn. The abrupt movements associated with windshield-wiper turns will often lead to imbalance. It is very important to realize that *speeding up and slowing down are natural functions of making turns.*

Banking vs. Angulation

There are two main ways to balance the outward forces created by turning. Banking (left) involves leaning the entire body into the direction of the turn. Notice that a significant amount of the skier's weight is riding on the inside ski—a potentially precarious situation. By contrast, angulating (right) involves leaning the hips and knees into the hill, while leaning the upper body into the skis. The result is the classic "banana" position, which keeps the weight well-balanced on the outside ski.

The *phases of the turn* give you a framework within which to consider acceleration, deceleration, and the other technical elements discussed up to this point.

The first phase is called *preparation*. At this point we are finishing the previous turn or going across the hill in a traverse. As the name implies, physical and mental anticipation happen during this phase.

In the second phase of the turn, the *initiation,* we change edges, begin to add rotary power, and possibly transfer our weight to the outside ski. Initiation can be made easier by lightening our skis. This is called "unweighting." We accomplish this in various ways such as by rapid up or down motions of our body, or by going over convex terrain on the ski slope. These and other methods of unweighting will be discussed in subsequent chapters. The initiation is often described, and felt, as the "light" phase of the turn.

The Parts of a Turn

All turns can be divided into
four parts:

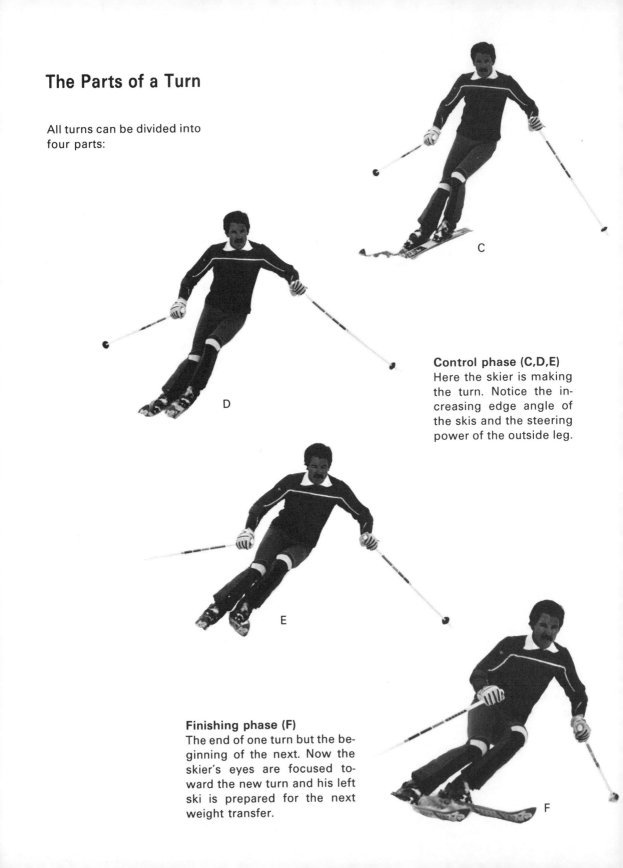

C

Control phase (C,D,E)
Here the skier is making
the turn. Notice the in-
creasing edge angle of
the skis and the steering
power of the outside leg.

D

E

Finishing phase (F)
The end of one turn but the beginning of the next. Now the
skier's eyes are focused toward the new turn and his left
ski is prepared for the next
weight transfer.

F

B

Initiation (B)
Weight transfer (or un-
weighting) by extension
of the legs (up-motion)
and the beginning of
edge change comprise
the second phase of the
turn.

A

Preparation (A)
The skier looks ahead—
never down at his skis—
in the direction of the
new turn.

In the third part of the turn, called the *control phase,* our weight gradually returns to the skis as we guide them through the desired arc. We do this by regulating edge angle, leverage, and rotary power. More inward lean is necessary to help tip the skis on a higher edge and to counteract increasing effects of centrifugal force.

The fourth and final part of the turn is called the *finishing phase.* Maximum edge angle and inward lean occur since the outward pull of centrifugal force is the greatest here. Our actions to resist this pull make this part of the turn feel the heaviest. As this phase is concluded, we begin to prepare for the next turn.

Along with all of the preceding technical considerations, we maintain balance by moving in accordance with changes in terrain. Ski slopes, in spite of excellent grooming, are not as smooth as billiards tables. To remain upright over the dips, bumps, and rolls inherent on the slopes, you must constantly readjust the body in the fore, aft, and lateral planes. Your sight, your inner ears, and the nerve endings in the soles of your feet are your primary sensors for gathering information about the changes to formulate responses to them.

EQUIPMENT AND ITS RELATIONSHIP TO TECHNIQUE

Ski equipment is in a constant state of refinement and there is a "chicken-or-egg" aspect to this evolution. Does new equipment cause changes in technique, or do new techniques cause changes in equipment? Whatever the answer, skiing is most certainly easier today because of the gear that is available.

Ski equipment is designed to complement the muscular actions that guide our bodies through turns and to help us work with the forces that are created in the process. The topic of ski mechanics is an extremely complex one, so this discussion will again be limited to the main points that are essential to understanding how we make turns down the mountain.

Skis and Skiing Technique

The ski itself is obviously at the center of any discussion about equipment as it relates to technique. Skis were originally invented thousands of years ago in Europe and Scandinavia to prevent winter travelers from sinking into the snow. They still perform this basic job, particularly in softer snow conditions. But relative to alpine technique, the basic role of the ski is in reducing the friction between your body and the snow to allow you to slide down the mountain. Since sliding creates speed and momentum, you have to perform the technical aspects of making turns, which were discussed earlier in this chapter.

A ski complements the muscular actions we use to make turns by its sidecut, which was defined in Chapter Two. When you tip the ski on edge to begin the process of deflection around the desired curve, the tip and tail of the ski tend to bite in harder because of the ski's hourglass shape. Since your weight is more or less in the center, the ski tends to bend into a curve because of this shape.

Sidecut can produce this curve because the ski has been engineered to have a controlled longitudinal stiffness. If the ski were as stiff as a two-by-four, no amount of sidecut would encourage it to bend into an arc. Fortunately, skis flex along their length, and the bent shape that the ski assumes allows the skier to make more-or-less rounded arcs in the process of turning. Skis with a softer longitudinal flex will bend into an arc quite easily. For this reason, soft skis are appropriate for the beginning skier, while skis that have very stiff flexes require progressively more weight, pressure, and technique to bend them into an arc. Expert skiers and racers often use skis of this sort because they have the ability to direct the combination of their weight and centrifugal force more accurately into the ski they are turning on. This ability allows them to create sufficient pressure to make stiffer skis bend into an arc.

Regardless of your ability level, as you tip the skis on edge to begin the turning process, the forces generated will try to flatten the skis out. A ski's torsional stiffness, which is the resistance to twisting along its longitudinal axis, counteracts this flattening. It allows the ski to maintain the arc that your movements, in concert with sidecut and longitudinal flex, have developed. As discussed in Chapter Two, beginning skis usually have softer torsional stiffness because they are easier to turn, and expert skis are stiffer in this regard. In explanation, because of the slower speeds of beginning skiers, they generally require lower edge angles, and consequently produce less force in the course of making turns. Expert skiers need more torsional rigidity because greater forces are created by their faster speeds and subsequently by the higher edge angles of their skis.

When you consider the interplay of sidecut, longitudinal flex, and torsional stiffness, you begin to understand how difficult it is to build skis. Different manufacturing techniques and materials are combined to produce skis that are appropriate for different levels of skier. Although there is some empirical data concerning sidecut radius and basic flex guidelines, many of a ski's characteristics are chosen and engineered into a ski quite subjectively. Ski testers are employed to determine whether a ski with all the right "numbers" feels right and will work for the ability level for which it was designed.

Boots and Skiing Technique

The primary job of the boot is to transmit turning power to the skis. In terms of rotary power, boots do this by conducting the torque produced by your muscles through the bindings, which, in turn, gets the skis moving in a curved path. This action is made possible because the boot surrounds your foot and has sufficient stiffness not to absorb and dissipate the rotary power you have created. In essence, the boot forms a link between the rotary, edging, and pressuring movements of your body and the skis.

One of the most important tasks the boot performs in this regard is supplying sufficient lateral strength to tip the ski on edge to begin the process of deflection. The boot does this thanks to its height and its resistance to sideways bending. Like the longitudinal or torsional flex in a ski, softer boots are more appropriate for beginning skiers. Beginners' boots often do not encounter large forces such as those produced by expert skiers. Because these boots are softer, they are also less sensitive to turning input from the skier. Detuning a recreational boot this way, however, makes skiing much easier for beginners because softer boots allow more freedom of ankle flex and hence better balance. Stiffer boots allow expert skiers to really tip their skis on edge

Ski boots transmit turning power to the skis—the boots' lateral strength allows you to turn the skis and tip them on edge to produce the kind of reverse camber shown here.

Even an advanced skier's boot provides a considerable amount of ankle-flex.

A

B

 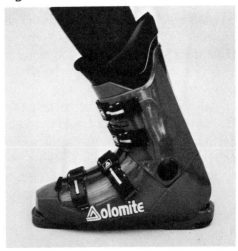

and to balance the forces created when they do this. Beginners do not make such radical movements intentionally.

The final job of a ski boot is to help the skier maintain balance over the skis. Because a boot is stiff in the fore and aft planes, it helps the skier catch himself from falling over backwards or forwards as he accelerates or decelerates. It also makes the use of leverage possible, since it blocks and transmits pressure to the skis. The paradox is that boot stiffness can help you maintain your balance but the leverage it provides may be the cause of imbalance in the first place.

Poles and Skiing Technique

Ski poles assist the skier in several ways. In a fundamental way they help him propel himself across flat areas of terrain. They also help the skier maintain balance. Like antennae, poles, when touched or dragged in the snow, can help you determine your relationship to the slope. Furthermore, dragging the poles is often the only way to remain upright under extremely bad visibility conditions, such as during a "whiteout" (caused by dense fog or blowing snow).In recreational skiing, poles also serve more sophisticated purposes. Use of the poles as timing and rhythm devices, as well as in mogul skiing, will be discussed at length in Chapter Six. Suffice it to say for now that your ski poles perform many important technical functions when you ski.

SKILLS CONCEPT

Many years ago, a great ski teacher from Stowe, Vermont, Cal Cantrell, told me something that absolutely confused me for some time. Cantrell said that if you took a head-on picture of a person doing a wedge turn and a shot from the same angle of someone doing a parallel turn, then cut both photos in half longitudinally, you wouldn't know which half was the parallel turn and vice versa.

After thinking about it for a time and observing people making these two types of turns—which will be discussed in subsequent chapters—it started to make sense. The outside leg eventually does exactly the same thing regardless of the sort of turn a skier makes. The only difference is the inside leg. In a wedge turn, the inside leg is allowed to hang to the inside in a training wheel sort of fashion. In parallel turns, the inside leg rides along more or less in alignment with the working outside leg. There's obviously a lot more to it than that, and

There is a thread of technical consistency that runs from the most basic to the most advanced turns. Notice the similarity between the basic body position of the skier doing a beginner's wedge turn (left) and the skier doing an advanced parallel turn (right). The right leg is doing exactly the same thing. The only difference is the position of the inside leg.

we'll get into the differences in turning forces in later chapters, but the statement is essentially true.

This observation is the fundamental principle behind the "skills approach," which was discussed in Chapter One. There is a thread of technical consistency that runs from a beginner's first turns to the most advanced skiing done by a World Cup racer. All skiers have to do certain basic things to turn their skis, and the only thing that changes is the sophistication of the movements. Keep this in mind as you read the next three chapters.

Your First Days on Skis

No matter how much preparation you do in advance, you're bound to feel nervous the first time you go skiing. This is a normal reaction. Everyone has a natural fear of the unknown, and skiing, like any other sport, takes learning and getting used to.

This chapter will take you step by step through your first days on the snow. As discussed in Chapter One, you should definitely take a lesson from a certified professional ski teacher. Learning from a friend is not acceptable. Skiing is too enjoyable a recreational activity to have yourself forever turned off, or possibly injured, as a result of incompetent instruction—however well-intentioned.

To insure your success with alpine skiing, many instructors—myself included—recommend that you also consider trying nordic skiing first. Nordic, or cross-country skiing as it is commonly known, will introduce you to the fundamentals in a very tame environment. Nordic centers also employ instructors who are certified by PSIA. By learning to move on cross-country skis, you'll begin to get a feel for sliding on snow. Nordic also provides an opportunity to learn climbing, basic turning skills, and the use of your ski poles. These are all things you'd otherwise learn in your first

75

Children remind us that we all can feel a bit tentative during our first few days on skis.

Cross-country skiing is an excellent way to pick up basic techniques for your first downhill skiing experience.

alpine skiing lesson, but nordic equipment is much lighter and easier to manage than alpine equipment. Cross-country centers also have very gentle terrain, so there is no fear of skiing out of control. After even a few hours on this sort of equipment, you could be assured of much faster learning on conventional alpine gear.

Before heading to the slopes for your first alpine skiing experience, you should do the following:

1) *Make sure you are going to an area with a ski school that teaches the American Teaching Method (ATM).* Stay away from places that promise to teach you with a "direct parallel," graduated-length method of instruction. Schools such as these begin their students on short skis and immediately try to teach them parallel turns. This approach is ineffective because it tries to teach you to run before you have learned to walk. Over the years I have worked with

many skiers who were the products of direct parallel schools. This microwave-oven approach to teaching develops skiers who look good at first glance but often go to pieces in challenging situations. The ATM, which also suggests a graduated-length method of instruction, produces students who progress quickly but develop their skills in a sensible, methodical fashion.

2) *Find out about the current skiing conditions at the area you'll be visiting.* In general, you'll progress faster if the weather conditions are decent your first time out. During your first day on skis, there's enough to contend with, without having to deal with severe snowstorms, glare ice, or heavy rain. But please don't use less-than-ideal conditions as an excuse to stay in the base lodge. Bad weather will bother you less as you become a more proficient skier. (For more information on determining ski conditions, consult appendix, page 187.)

3) *Plan on heading out to the ski school meeting place about 15 minutes before class is scheduled to begin.* This gives you an opportunity to get your equipment on, which may take some effort the first time. The other reason for getting there early is that most ski schools will start beginners classes (often called "A" Class) a few minutes early if there are enough students. Good ski school supervisors will group the first eight or ten people who are ready and immediately send an instructor over to begin working with them.

YOUR FIRST LESSON: THE BASICS

After the instructor meets everyone in the class, the first thing he or she will do is check out your equipment. This usually is not an overt thing: the teacher simply makes a visual scan of each skier's gear. If you are unsure about something—especially the functioning of your bindings—this is a good time to ask for help.

The teacher's next task is to help you get accustomed to your equipment. By donning boots and skis you have suddenly changed the weight and length of your feet. In a sense, your feet are at least five times longer and much heavier than normal, and this takes some getting used to. The best way to do it is to think of feet-plus-boots-plus-skis as big feet. The instructor will probably start you out with some basic exercises, such as lifting one ski up and twisting it, or walking around on flat terrain. As you do these exercises, remember that the skis are only an extension of the feet you've grown up with all your life. The more aware of this you can become, the more natural your first movements on skis will be. If you forget about it, and think of your feet without taking into consideration the extra length the skis have given them, the skis will end up crossing all the time and your movements will be awkward at best.

F

E

D

Sidestepping

After walking around on the level for a short period of time, you next need to move up the slope a short distance so you can learn how to slide. Unfortunately, the area where beginners start out doesn't usually have any sort of lift so you'll have to climb a little ways up the slope under your own power. The easiest way to climb on skis is by *sidestepping*. To sidestep, start by positioning your skis at a 90-degree angle to the fall-line (the line of least resistance down the mountain—the path a ball would travel if it rolled down the hill) and climb the hill by making a lateral step with the uphill ski, then lifting the downhill ski beside it. Your poles help provide balance in sidestepping, and as you move one ski up the hill, you move the corresponding pole at the same time.

Since your skis are edged slightly while sidestepping, you should feel a soft pressure along the *inside of your downhill foot* and the *outside of your uphill foot* as you step from ski to ski. Rather than getting hung up in the mechanics of this, you will find that the easiest way to learn how to sidestep is to watch the instructor and other people in the class doing it.

This is a good general rule to follow in a group ski lesson. The ski teacher has been trained to provide you with the most accurate visual image possible. Try to cue in on the instructor's movements, and simply imitate them. The other students in the class are also a tremendous learning tool. By listening to the feedback the teacher gives them, you can avoid their mistakes and duplicate their success. If everyone in the class has this awareness, the group will progress much faster.

C

B

A

Sidestepping
The skier attains the necessary grip for climbing the hill by edging her skis slightly.

The Herringbone

Another useful technique that you should learn for climbing slopes is the traditional *herringbone*. Start by facing the slope and opening your skis so that the tips are apart, the tails together—in other words, in sort of a reverse wedge position. With your poles behind you for support and the heels of your hands on top of the grips, roll your ankles slightly so that your weight is on the *inside* edges of your skis and start cutting steps up the slope. Your pole plants should be firm and vigorous; you should push back on the pole opposite the stepping foot. Keep your head up and your back straight, put your weight on the *inside* edge of the stepping ski, and don't lean too far forward or you'll start slipping backwards. If the slope steepens, just widen your reverse wedge for extra purchase.

When you reach the top of the slope, look back: you should see the fish-skeleton pattern from which the herringbone name originates.

The Herringbone
This is another traditional method for climbing slopes. The skier keeps her poles behind her and her hands on top of the grips for added leverage.

Straight Running

Probably, the first actual skiing maneuver the instructor will introduce is *straight running.* Don't worry about going too fast: You haven't climbed very far up the hill. Just be sure there is a natural outrun—a place where the slope flattens out—so you'll gradually come to a stop. (In the case of an area without a natural outrun, don't worry: The teacher will already have taught you how to make gradual steps in one direction so you can stop yourself.)

Straight running is your first introduction to the real joy of skiing: sliding on snow. Balance in motion is what skiing is all about. The position for a straight run is similar to the movement-ready stance used in such sports as tennis, hockey, and basketball. All of the joints of the body are relaxed and slightly flexed. When you watch the teacher demonstrate, notice that the body is basically perpendicular to the skis. Thousands of small muscle firings are required to maintain this posture, but if you let yourself relax, it's easy.

One of the best hints for doing a good straight run is to try to have full contact with the soles of your feet in the ski boots (that is, you should feel pressure on the entire sole of your foot—heel, arch, and ball). You want to center your weight in the middle of the skis. To help you learn this, the instructor might have you stand in a level area and rock back and forth with your eyes closed. The goal is to home in on standing with your weight on the entire foot. If you observe another student going through this process, you'll notice that his body always ends up being fairly perpendicular to his skis.

Straight running is also facilitated by holding the hands forward and away from the body, and looking ahead. *Don't constantly look down at your skis!* This latter point is extremely important. From the outset you should learn to feel

Straight running
All body joints are slightly flexed, the arms are up and forward for better balance, and the skier is looking ahead in the direction he is going.

the interaction between skis and snow, instead of looking down to see it. Looking ahead and staying kinesthetically sensitive is the most effective way to maintain balance on skis.

The teacher may introduce several exercises at this point to help you become better balanced while straight running. You might be asked to lift one ski, then the other, to flex down low, then extend tall; or to hop the skis off the snow as you're going along in the straight run. Whatever exercises are chosen, the goal is to improve your balance on a sliding ski.

The Gliding Wedge

Once the class looks fairly stable in the straight run, the next thing to learn is a *gliding wedge,* which many veteran skiers still refer to as the *snowplow.* Most instructors will have you push or hop your skis into this wedge pattern while standing in a level area before having you try it in motion. When the skis are in this configuration, they are tipped very slightly onto their inside edges. To get into this position, use exactly the same stance as in the straight run, but move the tails of the skis farther apart than the tops. As you move down the hill in a wedge, think of making an "A," with the skis as the outsides of the letter, and your hips as the crossbar.

The reason for learning the wedge right away is that it is a natural position

The gliding wedge
This is the same basic stance as in the straight run, but the tails of the skis are wider apart than the tips and ride slightly on their inside edges.

The snowplow
The tails of the skis are much more widely displaced than in the gliding wedge. This is a difficult position to turn from because the skis are edged so severely.

to make turns from. As noted in Chapter Three, edge change is the most fundamental aspect of making turns. In a wedge, both edges are changed—the right ski is ready for a left turn, and the left ski is ready for a right turn. Today we teach a narrow gliding wedge, instead of the very wide snowplow of years past, because it offers the advantage of preparing both skis for turns without putting them on such high edge angles that they are difficult to turn.

Maintaining your skis in this position is quite simple. Once you have displaced the tails with some muscular effort, they remain there so long as you keep *your weight in the middle of the wedge.* Keep your weight centered on the skis from front to back (as you did in the straight run), since this will prevent them from crossing one another.

The teacher may have you do several exercises to help improve your dexterity with the wedge. Wedge change-ups (going from a straight run to a wedge, to a straight run, and back again), hopping the skis into a wedge while moving, and going from a gliding wedge to a wider, braking wedge are a few that you might be exposed to. If you are taught to do a braking wedge, try not to rely on it too much for slowing down. It is much better to make turns to slow down, and you will learn this next.

Wedge Turns

If you can maintain a balanced gliding wedge, making wedge turns is simple. In fact, the first turns you make from a wedge are often referred to as "magic turns" because there is no visible reason for them to happen. To perform these slight deflections from the fall-line, gently point your feet in one direction, then the other. It is just that easy. The products of this muscular effort are very gradual turns down the mountain.

The common pitfall in these initial attempts to turn is trying too hard. You'll want to get your entire body involved in the process, when you only need to use your legs. Think about making round, "S-shaped" turns and imagine that your feet are standing on the steering wheel of a bus and you are turning them (and the wheel) in the direction you want to go. Zorro turns (named for their sharp-edged Z shape) will get you into trouble because abrupt changes of direction disturb your balance.

Another common problem is putting the ski on too high an edge by skiing in a braking wedge. Closely related to this is forcefully driving your knee into the turn. In either case it is difficult to make the skis turn because the edges are gripping the snow too hard. Stand in the middle of a narrow wedge, and guide the skis through gentle turns with your legs.

To make more pronounced turns, all you have to do is guide the skis in

C

B

A

D

The Wedge Turn

If you can stay balanced in the center of a gliding wedge, all you have to do is keep pointing your feet in the direction you want to go.

E

F

one direction for a longer period. Don't worry about creating bigger edge angles or trying consciously to weight your outside ski. More edge angle and weight on the outside ski are a natural function of staying balanced in a bigger turn. It is far easier for the teacher to ask you to add a bit more edge or weight than to unscrew you from the pretzel shape you will assume if you try to add too much to a basic turn.

Your ski teacher will be talking about *inside and outside skis* frequently during the course of the lesson. These terms speak of the skis' relationship to the radius of your turn. If you are turning to the left, the left ski is the inside one and the right ski is the outside one. In a right turn it is just the opposite.

Riding the Lift

Once the instructor determines that the class can make turns in both directions you'll go to the ski lift. Thank heaven, because climbing up and down the hill can be a tiring experience for both student and instructor. You might think after all the above discussion that riding the lift won't happen for days ("so much to learn before that!"), but usually you will be heading up the lift about one hour after the class has started. Some classes need more time; others will go up a bit sooner.

Riding a ski lift is easy. There are many different types of lifts, but most areas use slow-moving chairlifts that are strung low to the ground for their beginner slopes. It is no problem getting on and off any ski lift, provided that you listen to the instructor's suggestions carefully and follow these basic rules. First, take off your pole straps and hold both poles in one hand (which hand is determined by the type of chair you're riding—the instructor or the lift operator will tell you). When it's your turn, shuffle on to the loading ramp and look over your inside or outside shoulder (again it depends on the type of chair). Watch as the chair approaches, and try to time your sitting down to the moment when the chair just reaches you.

Once you're on the lift, sit back, pull down the chair's safety bar (a metal bar that drops in front of you at chest level to prevent you from falling out), relax, and enjoy the ride to the top. Be careful to hold on to your poles, and if you need to get something out of your pocket, let your partner hold the poles for you. Occasionally the lift will stop in the course of your ride to the top. This happens when people weren't ready at the loading or unloading areas, and occasionally when dictated by mechanical reasons. No matter how long the lift is stopped, don't even *think* about jumping out of the chair—you might injure yourself. If there is a serious problem with the lift, the ski patrol will come by to give assistance or to help evacuate you if necessary (an unusual occurrence, believe me!).

Riding the Lift

A

Getting on the lift

When getting on a lift, hold your poles in one hand, wait for the chair before yours to go by, then shuffle to the loading area (usually marked by a board) and turn backwards (A). The hand nearest the oncoming chair should be free to grasp the arm railing (NOTE: If the chair has an arm divider between the seats, turn so that you can grasp that bar). When the chair reaches you, grasp the arm rail and sit (B). Then lower the safety bar (C) and ride. You should hold your poles firmly inside the safety bar (D).

A

B

B

C

D

Getting off the lift

When preparing to get off the lift, raise the safety bar at the designated location, put your poles in one hand, and check to make sure that none of your clothing has become tangled in the chair (A). As you near the unloading platform, keep your ski tips up and move to the edge of the chair (B). Once you are over the platform, let your skis make contact with the ground (C). Then, grasping the chair in one hand, push away from it at the unloading point (D) and ski to the left or right down the platform (E) to make room for the next skiers. Stop by doing a snowplow.

C

D

E

Ordinarily you'll ride to the top without stopping. Signs are always posted on lift towers telling you when to prepare to unload at the lift's upper terminal. Before you get there, check to make sure that neither your ski poles nor your clothing has become entangled in the chair. Wait until you get to the sign at the terminal telling you to stand up, and let yourself slide down the unloading ramp.

Many people fall down on these ramps because they haven't made an adjustment from the flat place where they initially stood up to the unloading ramp's gentle incline. Remember, as you learned in the straight run, that *the body has to be perpendicular to the skis to remain in balance.* Since the ramp slopes down slightly, you have to tilt your entire body forward so that it remains at a 90-degree angle to your skis.

After you make it down the unloading ramp, move a short distance away from it so that you aren't in the way of other skiers. Wait there as the rest of your ski class assembles. The instructor usually rides up the lift last, and once he gets there you are ready to begin applying your newly learned skills.

YOUR FIRST LESSON: ON THE BEGINNERS' SLOPE

Try to remember as you look down the beginners' slope that it is not as steep as it appears. In most cases, by the end of your first day—and certainly by the end of the second—you will be anxious to ski more challenging terrain. Be confident that you know how to make a basic wedge turn and that if you keep turning in one direction, you'll eventually come to a stop. As in your first turns down on the super-flat, class "A" area, the key is *not to rush your movements.* You have some very big feet now, and you have to be patient to get them to turn.

If at any time you get out of control and can't regain your composure, the best thing to do is sit down to the outside of either ski if you're going straight down the slope, or on the uphill side if you're going across the hill. Remember: The best-padded place on the human anatomy is the derriere, so use yours to cushion your fall. Skiers get injured by sticking vulnerable parts of their body, especially the knees, into the snow to break their fall.

There are many ways to get back up after you fall down. With more experience, you simply get up, but for the beginning skier it isn't always that easy. Other than being helped by someone else, the best way to get up after a fall is first to roll over so you're lying flat on your stomach, with your knees flexed at a 90-degree angle. Rotate one leg outward, then the other, so the skis form a "V" (tails together, tips apart), with your body in the center. To get up, simply push up as you "walk" your hands back toward your feet. As you stand

Falling

If you fall down, don't land on a vulnerable part of your body the way the skier above is doing. Try to land to the sides of your skis on the ample padding of your buttocks, and keep your poles out to your sides (below).

up, lift one ski beside the other, so you are standing across the fall-line. Once you brush off the snow and put your skis back on if they released, you're ready to go.

Even if you didn't fall during your first run down the beginners' slope, your performance was probably a bit tentative. The teacher probably set a track for you to follow and may have given you feedback about your performance. If there were problems, again it probably came in the form of overdoing it. I can't stress this enough—it's easy to turn a pair of skis on a smooth, perfectly groomed beginners' slope. Let your legs do the turning and your upper body will be free to maintain balance on the sliding skis.

In most cases, you'll probably have time to take another run before the class is over. This run will mostly be a chance for you to get some skiing miles under your belt, and little if any new material will be introduced. At this point the teacher is trying to help you get comfortable on the skis and to ingrain memory patterns in your muscles. The teacher will always assemble the class at the bottom of the slope for a brief review and possibly for additional individual feedback.

When the class is over you might wonder if it's appropriate to give the instructor a "tip." If the teacher was especially helpful, by all means feel free to give him something. Ski teachers really appreciate your generosity, but remember that a gratuity is the exception, not the rule. If you've had an exceptionally good or bad lesson, bring it to the attention of the ski school supervisor.

After class, you will probably want to go inside the base lodge to relax and get something to eat. Keep in mind the suggestions on nutrition I'll be making later, and try to ingest complex carbohydrates as much as possible. Also remember to drink lots of fluids, as you have probably lost more in the past two hours than you think. But stay away from alcoholic beverages, at least until the end of the day. Drinking and skiing are potentially as dangerous as drinking and driving. Don't let your friends tell you that a drink will loosen you up and make you ski better. It won't.

After a break of at least an hour, you'll be ready to venture out on the slopes by yourself. Many ski areas offer an additional two-hour class lesson in the afternoon with their beginners' package, but I don't recommend it. Usually it is much better to practice in the afternoon, rather than overload yourself with new skills. Plus, it's nice to have the afternoon free to ski with a friend who's learning, without any external pressure.

Stay on the beginners' runs while you're practicing. These areas are marked with trail signs bearing a green circle above the word "Easiest" in large letters. As you ski these runs, try to establish a turning rhythm. Say "Turn,

turn, turn . . ." to yourself in an even, easy cadence.

As you become more confident and start to ski down the slope slightly faster, your inside leg will begin to turn in beside the outside leg toward the end of each turn. This is especially true if you are in a narrow wedge. If you feel this happening, *don't discourage it!* When your skis assume this relationship toward the end of the turn, you have discovered a key aspect of upper-level skiing—turning on corresponding, rather than opposing, edges. This form of turn is called a *christy.*

During a wedge turn most of your turning power is coming from the inside edge of the outside ski. That is, you are turning on the right edge of the left ski when turning to the right, and the left edge of the right ski when turning left. The inside ski is relatively flat on the snow, and its main function is to act as the fulcrum for the rotary power of the other leg. In a sense, one leg turns around the other as you make wedge turns down the hill.

When the inside leg comes alongside the outside leg toward the end of the turn, both skis are either on their right or left edges. The advantage of this "basic christy" is that you now have both edges working to help control your speed and to guide your body through the desired turn radius.

In the next several ski classes you will learn to refine this christy phase. The instructor will introduce such exercises as hockey stops, easy race courses, and others to help you learn to regulate the amount of edge needed to make different turn radii. During these exercises it is important to be aware of the soles of your feet. Begin consciously to feel the inside of your foot (the same place you felt while sidestepping) as you make turns.

If you can achieve this kinesthetic awareness, you are beginning to carry more weight on the outside ski. *Weight transfer must become a conscious act at this point for your skiing skills to improve further.* Gentle skating steps and lifting up one ski are a few of the exercises you might be asked to do in your next few classes to help learn to balance with more weight on one ski. The simple rule to remember is that you want to *have your weight on the right ski to turn left, and on the left ski to turn right.*

The process of learning everything we have covered to this point has probably taken a maximum of three days. That's the most remarkable thing about learning to ski. Sure, there are many other entertaining sports, but very few allow for the rapid skill acquisition that skiing does. And, if you apply the training and visualizing approaches that I'll discuss in Chapter Seven, you will probably have little difficulty moving into intermediate and advanced skills. Most important about all this is that the basic skills you are using now are the same as those used by the very best skiers in the world—only the degree of sophistication is different.

The Basic Christy

B

A

The skier starts by stemming the tail of his
right ski uphill (A,B,C). As he turns left (D,E),
his inside (left) ski gradually becomes parallel to the outside ski (F). When this happens,
the uphill edges of both skis help control
the speed and radius of the turn (G,H,I).

H

I

5

Intermediate Skiing

Intermediate skiing ranges from doing the basic christy, which we discussed at the end of the last chapter, to being able to make good parallel turns. As you read this chapter, keep in mind that the *maneuvers* you learn as an intermediate are not the main issue. What you are doing is acquiring the *skills* necessary to handle more challenging terrain and snow conditions. The acquisition of these skills merely manifests itself in maneuvers that ski technicians identify with certain jargon. So don't worry about the terminology. It is the fundamentals of edging, rotary power, and pressure control which we'll put into action here that are the real issues.

In acquiring these skills you need mileage, *lots of it.* The more you ski, the better balanced and more natural your skiing movements will become. But as you seek mileage, remember: *Perfect practice makes perfect.* If you practice improper movements, you will get better only at doing the wrong thing.

That's why so many skiers develop bad habits during this phase of their development. Most people have more than adequate athletic ability to become better skiers, but they stop taking lessons and try to learn by doing it by themselves and

95

The best way to progress as an intermediate skier is
. . . to ski.

watching others. That's fine if there are good skiers around you to imitate and you understand what you're seeing, but you can develop some extremely odd movement patterns this way, and these can be difficult to unlearn. There is no sense in slowing your progress with poor practice, so try to get feedback along the way. The best way to do that is to take consecutive lessons, such as those provided by a ski week. If you decide to use the drills and exercises discussed in this chapter to teach yourself, make sure you check in with a professional who can give you direction along the way.

EXERCISES, DRILLS, AND TECHNIQUES FOR IMPROVING THE BASIC CHRISTY

As discussed in the previous chapter, the basic christy begins with a wedge turn and finishes with the skis turned parallel to each other. This brief skidded phase, in which you draw your skis together and finish the turn, allows you to use the edges of both skis to control your speed and your turn radius. Since even the very top levels of skiing involve some sort of skidding action while turning, developing good fundamentals at this stage is essential.

Your goal should be to control the skid so that the turn shape is appropriate for a given situation. Some slopes require a sharp turn where the skis really get across the hill, leaving a fish-hook shaped trail in the snow); other slopes require you to make long, gradual turns that move a long ways down the fall-line and leave a trail like a big, flat "S." In between these patterns are a wide range of different turns. Each is accomplished by regulating the intensity and duration of rotary power and the degree of edging, and by manipulating where and how much pressure is applied to the skis.

As you enter this realm of skiing, the design of your skis becomes increasingly important. Making turns now requires angling your skis so that they turn on a *working edge*. Once you can achieve this, side-cut and torsional/longitudinal flex both begin to assist you in making turns.

One of the first things to consider to improve your basic christy is the pressure along the inside of your foot. Be sensitive to this area as you finish a turn. If you have a pair of ski boots handy, you can get the feel for foot pressure without even being on the snow. Stand with your feet about hip-width apart and the soles of the boots flat on the floor. Now gradually roll one boot onto its inside edge. Do you feel some sort of pressure along the ball of your foot, your arch, and your heel? Where is it more pronounced? Can you first pressure the ball, then move the pressure back to the heel? Do the same on the other foot.

Traversing

To traverse properly, make sure you remain upright over the downhill ski. Note how the downhill ski rides on its inside edge.

When you get on the snow with skis, try the following game of kinesthetic awareness. Begin by going across the hill in a straight run. This is called *traversing,* and it's an excellent way to develop edging skills. As you move across the hill, try to keep your weight on your *downhill ski* and concentrate on maintaining pressure along the *inside* of your foot. By experimenting, you'll find that a shallow traverse—one that is more perpendicular to the fall-line—results in slower speeds. You'll also find that a steep traverse—one that is more down the hill—results in higher speeds. Shallow traverses make you feel most comfortable at first, but you have to challenge yourself. Speed makes turning easier.

Steeper traverses

Try steeper traverses (A), which result in higher speeds. To stop, finish each traverse with a christy that turns you into the hill (B,C,D).

At the end of your traverse, do a basic christy, then focus again on the *inside of your downhill foot*. What you are learning is a slightly more sophisticated form of edge control. To do it properly, make sure you remain *upright* over the downhill ski. You cannot maintain the necessary resistance from the edge to hold your traverse by leaning into the hill. The body position that results from remaining upright over the downhill ski helps you learn an angular relationship with the skis that becomes ever more important as your skiing progresses.

Sideslipping

As an added exercise at this point, try some basic *sideslipping* to help you achieve greater edging dexterity. From the holding traverse we practiced above, gently reduce the amount of your skis' edge angle. Once you have flattened the edges sufficiently so that the skis no longer can resist your weight, you will begin to slip down the hill sideways. Let it happen! The easiest way to reduce edge angle is to slowly extend your legs and upper body. Play with going from a holding traverse to a short sideslip, back to a holding traverse. Be sure to do this in both directions.

A

B

C

Sideslipping
From a holding traverse (A), roll the skis so that they are flat on the snow. This produces a sideslip (B). To stop, simply roll the skis onto their uphill edges (C). Sideslipping is an excellent exercise for improving edge awareness.

Pedaling

After you have a feel for the edging skills required to make a good traverse, you need to get better at weight transfer. One of the easiest exercises for learning good weight transfer is to go across the hill in a holding traverse, but make a pedaling motion with your legs. Lift one ski, then the other, first doing it rhythmically, with a definite walking motion, then trying to balance for a short time on either leg. You should find it easier to balance on the downhill ski.

Pedaling
As an exercise to improve your balance in the traverse, try lifting the uphill ski (top) then the downhill ski (bottom) in different cadences.

Skating Steps

Another good exercise for improving weight transfer skills is doing simple *skating steps.* These are also useful for propelling yourself across sections of the mountain that are too gradual for sliding. Learn them in the flats or on a very gradual pitch. If you recall the image of Eric Heiden ice skating in the 1980 Olympics, you'll find that the movement on skis is very similar. You move by pushing laterally off the inside edge of one ski to the outside edge of the other ski. To skate back onto the other foot, all you have to do is roll the ski you are standing on over onto its inside edge and push off. As you perform this simple skating step, again be aware of the *pressure* along the inside of the foot as you push off one ski to the other. The better the grip you can supply with this inside edge, the more propulsion you'll gain as you transfer the glide onto the other ski. Since you can emphasize either edging or weight transfer by skating, it's a versatile exercise and an excellent indicator of overall skill level. We will refer to skating steps several times in the chapter on advanced skiing.

Skating steps
Skating on the level is an easy way to improve your balance and get used to pushing off from one ski and gliding on the other.

A

B

C

D

E

F

G

H

I

J

K

Hockey Stops

Another multipurpose exercise, which will also improve the quality of your skidded phase, is the *hockey stop.* You do one almost exactly as you would on ice skates, except it's much easier on skis. Again you might find it useful to stand up wherever you are reading this and try the following exercise: Either in your street shoes, or your boots if they're handy, try to turn both legs in one direction. If you attempt this with your legs squeezed close together, you'll find that it is very difficult. Reason: The rotator muscles in your legs work much better when they are slightly apart. Georges Joubert, the French ski technician, first described this powerful form of leg rotation as "braquage."

When you try making a hockey stop for the first time on snow, do it from a shallow traverse. Going across the fall-line in a traverse, simply turn both legs into the hill. With experimentation, you'll find that it is much easier if you keep your weight centered on the downhill ski. After you've done one in the other direction from a shallow traverse, gradually make the traverse slightly steeper. Eventually you should be able to make your hockey stops from a traverse angle of nearly 45 degrees to the fall-line.

After you've done several of these exercises, go back and try doing basic christies again. The turns should feel more deliberate and controlled because you have improved all the skills necessary to make them. If you are having trouble getting the skis to "match" (that is, come together parallel to each other) at the end of the turn, try to apply the weight transfer skills you learned in the preceding exercises. Consciously keep your weight on the outside (turning) ski and you'll find that the inside leg will come in very easily. The earlier you can get the inside ski lightened (or *unweighted*), the easier it is to begin the skidded phase.

Another problem that often develops as you try to match the skis is attempting to drag it in on its downhill edge. This is called "catching the edge" of the inside ski, and it will not allow you to achieve the matching you are working on. For the skis to match successfully, the inside ski must be flat or rolled slightly on its uphill edge. That happens either as a natural function of inward lean in the turn, or through a conscious effort on your part to roll your inside knee up the hill. Doing skating steps required a similar movement as you rolled from an outside to an inside edge to push off. Try to apply this rolling movement as you match the skis toward the end of the turn.

There are many exercises and games you can begin at this point to further enhance your skidding and turn-shaping skills. One of the easiest is simply to follow another skier. Try to keep your skis going in exactly the same track as his. By doing this, you learn more about regulating the basic skills to produce

A

B

The Hockey stop
When the skier wants to stop traversing across the fall-line, he simply turns his legs
—and thus, the tips of his skis—into the hill (A), keeping his weight centered on his
downhill ski. Result: He stops (B)!

different turn shapes. Next, try making your skis follow an imaginary path
down the slope. Both of these methods are visual approaches to learning how
to change the size of the turn.

There are also several auditory approaches to changing turn radius. One
is to count while you are pressuring the outside ski. Stay on the turning ski,
counting one, two, three, four, five, then release the pressure, and do a five-
count on the other foot. Vary the count to create turns of different sizes.

Another auditory approach is to say "yah" as you stand on the turning
ski. Try contrasting turns where you say "Yaah, yaah, yaah" to turns where
you say "Yaaaaah, yaaaaah, yaaaaah." Associate the sound you are making
with the pressure build-up in the turn. In short turns the pressure build-up is
rapid and has a quick cadence; longer turns are just the opposite. This game
has an added benefit of forcing you to exhale while you're skiing. As we'll see
later, this is very important to provide the necessary fuel to allow the muscles
to fire effectively.

104   At this point it is fun to begin running some easy race courses. They will help you make turns in specific locations and better control your skis. Most ski classes will incorporate gates at this point, but if you're not in a class try joining in on easy fun races sponsored by the ski area. Many places will have their NASTAR (the National Standard Race) on relatively easy slopes, and this will give you an opportunity to go through the gates. When you participate in NASTAR you are given a handicap, which is based on the pacesetter's time. By keeping track of this, you have an objective criterion against which to judge your progress. More information about NASTAR and basic racing technique is contained in the following chapter.

How to Use Your Ski Poles

By now you may have begun to use your ski poles in the course of turning. That's great, but there a few things you should be aware of so you don't pick up bad habits. First, ski poles are like turn indicators—you plant the left for a left turn, the right for a right turn. To prepare the pole for placement into the snow, cock your wrist, thereby angling the pole slightly forward. (Since in a good basic stance your hands are held slightly forward and away from the body, you shouldn't have to involve your entire arm in the process.) Now touch the pole in the snow, and bring your skis parallel to each other as you skid through the finish of the turn. By repeating this rhythmically from one turn to another, you improve your timing and balance and develop a kinesthetic cue for when to skid.

Putting It All Together

Now put all of the preceding suggestions together into a stem christy. From a holding traverse, displace the tail of the uphill ski by pushing it up the hill. If there's a little weight on the ski you stemmed, it will begin deflecting you in the direction you want to go. As you turn toward the fall-line, begin consciously to transfer your weight to the stemmed ski. Get your pole ready to place in the snow, and when you plant it, match your skis (bring them parallel to each other) and control the skidded phase that you've created. After trying a turn in the other direction, begin linking turns together. Do it rhythmically. Say to yourself, "Turn! turn! turn!" or, 'Yaah! yaah! yaah!" By changing the cadence, you will create different shapes of turns.

Use of Ski Poles and Auditory Cues

Try planting a ski pole and saying, "Yaah!" at the start of each turn to help you develop the cadence for linking together short-radius turns. Remember: Plant the left pole for left turns, the right pole for right turns.

"Yaah!"

A

B

"Yaah!"

C

OTHER "INTERMEDIATE" TECHNIQUES

Converging Step Turns

Converging step turns are basically a tuned-up version of the stem christy. Their name derives from the skis' movement: By displacing the tail of the uphill ski, you put it into a position where it is pointing toward the ski you are standing on. Although I'm calling these intermediate-level turns, they have a wide range of sophistication. The best racers in the world use converging step turns as part of their racing arsenal, and you will be able to use them throughout your skiing development.

Converging step turns, or "stem steps" as they are often called, differ from stem christies mainly in how deliberately you commit to the stemmed ski. In a stem christy, you stem the uphill ski and gradually allow your weight to transfer to it as you move toward the fall-line. In a converging step turn, you transfer your weight immediately to the stemmed ski, well before the fall-line.

Try doing some stem steps on a well-groomed slope that you feel comfortable on. As you finish one turn, keep all your weight on the turning ski, lift the uphill ski, and point it in the direction you want to go. Engage the edge of that stemmed ski very softly in the snow and commit your weight to it. All you have to do at this point is balance on the edge of the converging ski, add a bit of rotary power if necessary to further direct the ski, and you'll make the turn.

Converging step turns are useful for a number of reasons. They improve the quality of the edging, rotary, and pressuring movements you use to turn the skis, and they can also help you on race courses or on bumps, where they provide a quick means to start a turn.

Converging Step Turns

To do a converging step turn from a traverse (A), start by stemming your uphill ski and deliberately unweighting your downhill ski (B,C). You carve the turn on your weighted uphill ski (D) while adding balance with the outside edge of your downhill ski (E). Now add a bit of rotary power from your legs and finish the turn with your skis parallel (F,G).

Diverging Step Turns

D

E

F

G

H

I

J

C   B   A

To do a diverging step turn, start from a fairly steep traverse (A). Push off of your downhill ski (B) and transfer your weight to the diverging uphill ski (C). Now extend the leg you have transferred your weight to (D) and gradually roll that uphill ski onto its inside edge (E,F), bring the unweighted ski parallel to it (G), and complete the turn with rotary and edge movements as necessary (H,I,J).

Diverging Steps

Diverging step turns are the opposite. Often referred to as "GS (or Giant Slalom) Steps," diverging step turns involve movements very similar to those you practiced when skating on the flats. If you are going to try some, find a gradual slope and first review skating from ski to ski.

To put this movement into a turn, start from a fairly steep traverse. Push off your downhill ski and transfer your weight to the diverging, uphill ski. Now, extend the leg you have transferred your weight to and gradually roll that uphill ski onto its inside edge, completing the turn with rotary and edge movement as necessary.

Learning how to do diverging steps will improve your skiing in many different ways. The pushoff from the downhill ski requires good edge engagement, and the skills involved with that are important in creating a solid platform (or base) with which to start a turn. You also improve both your weight-transfer skills and the way you use your legs to tip and turn the skis. Finally, this turn has direct applications for recreational racing, which we'll cover in the next chapter.

With the skills you've acquired so far, you should be able to handle "More Difficult" slopes at most ski areas. As you become more confident, you might even want to try some "Most Difficult" runs if they are well-groomed. If you take a ski week, or a consecutive lesson package through your local ski area, you can probably reach this level of skiing expertise by the fifth session.

The Parallel Turn

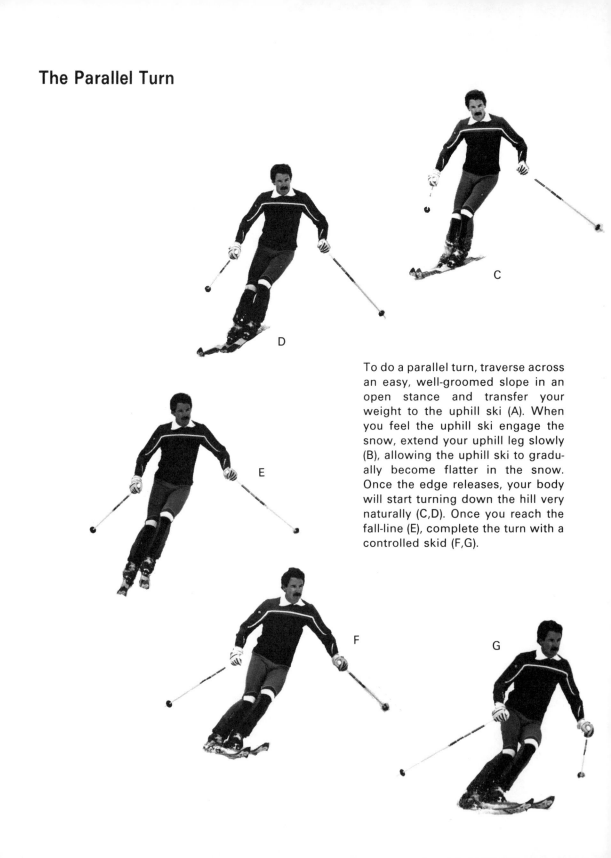

To do a parallel turn, traverse across an easy, well-groomed slope in an open stance and transfer your weight to the uphill ski (A). When you feel the uphill ski engage the snow, extend your uphill leg slowly (B), allowing the uphill ski to gradually become flatter in the snow. Once the edge releases, your body will start turning down the hill very naturally (C,D). Once you reach the fall-line (E), complete the turn with a controlled skid (F,G).

B

A

"PARALLEL SKIING"

"Parallel skiing" is a misnomer. In a pure sense, the parallel turn does not exist
—it is virtually impossible to maintain equal distance between the skis throughout a curve. Unfortunately, many skiers feel frustrated because they just can't
keep their skis parallel. If you are one of these, don't worry—the relationship
is elusive at best.

Rather than trying to maintain the skis in an impossible position, think
of "parallel" as referring to turn initiation. All the turns we've learned so far
have been started with a "one-two" type of movement. Ski technicians call this
sequential turn initiation. Remember? In the stem christy, by displacing the tail
of the uphill ski (one), you change edge to get going in the direction you want
to go. Then you steer toward the fall-line in a wedge and bring the inside ski
next to the outside ski (two) to complete the turn.

In parallel skiing, you start the turn with a simultaneous movement.
Simply put, you turn both skis at once. Learning to do this is really no big deal.
In fact, you probably did it spontaneously when you linked basic christies
together in a quick cadence. To make these turns consciously, you need to apply
the same principles that govern all turns. Change edges, apply some sort of
rotary power, and, ideally, weight the outside ski.

There are a number of ways to become more proficient at making parallel turns. One of the easiest is to link basic christies together as previously mentioned. If they are done with a quick, rhythmic cadence close to the fall-line, chances are you'll end up making wide-track, parallel turns. Don't worry that your feet aren't together. Your stance will gradually get narrower as you become more comfortable making parallel turns.

On the subject of stance width, it's okay to ski with some light showing between your legs. Gone are the days when ski teachers used to have you hold a dollar bill between your knees to teach you to glue your legs together. It is much easier and more efficient to ski with a slightly open stance. Your goal is to have the legs working as independent shock absorbers, rather than welded together as a mono shock.

An easy way to learn parallel turning skills is to traverse across the hill in an open stance. Make sure you're on a well-groomed slope that is not too challenging. Transfer your weight to the uphill ski, and feel that ski's uphill edge engage the snow. Now extend your uphill leg slowly, allowing the ski that you're standing on to gradually become flatter on the snow. Once that edge releases, your body will start turning down the hill very naturally if you have faith. Once you reach the fall-line, complete the turn with a controlled skid. *Voilà.* You have made your first parallel turn.

After you've tried this from a traverse in the other direction, begin to link one turn to another with a rhythmical cadence. Use the same auditory cues as you did to change the radii of your basic christies. If you have trouble with the movements required to link the turns together, find a very gradual slope and work more on skating from ski to ski. Skating onto the uphill edge of one ski, then rolling it over to the inside edge so that you can push off of it, is almost exactly the same movement your legs make in parallel turns.

Besides doing them rhythmically, you'll find it much easier to link parallel turns together if you have a definite base, or platform as it's called, from which to transfer your weight. To achieve a good platform you need to get good edge engagement toward the end of the previous turn. That can happen only if you have your weight directed firmly onto your downhill ski by having the body in an angulated position, or "banana shape" (discussed in Chapter Three).

Your ski poles can facilitate edge engagement. Try planting the pole well down the hill, at the very end of the skidded phase. Note that you must prepare for this pole plant by gradually cocking your wrist throughout the end of the turn. Don't just stick the pole into the snow at the very end. Swing the pole in concert with the entire turn. Don't make it an afterthought. When done properly, the pole's placement in the snow signals the end of one turn, the beginning of the next.

Proper pole placement keeps your weight balanced on the downhill ski and promotes better edge engagement.

APPLYING TECHNIQUE TO TERRAIN AND SNOW CONDITIONS

Learning to ski would be even easier if the surface we skied on was always the same. Unfortunately, ski slopes are not ice skating rinks or billiards tables. Groomed runs may approach the consistency of other playing surfaces, but by and large the reality of skiing is a constantly changing terrain and snow conditions. To progress through the intermediate levels of skiing and beyond, you must learn to adapt to variable surfaces and challenging conditions. Both test your balance, which will improve your overall stance on the skies. They also encourage you to move with more grace and fluidity, since they demand more finesse in applying the basic turning skills. Even though you might prefer staying on smooth, flat runs most of the time, you'll enjoy skiing even more if you get into some of the following examples of situational learning.

To improve your parallel skiing, it's important to challenge yourself on steeper and steeper slopes.

Ski Steeper Slopes

Some of the best challenges to begin with are steeper slopes. I don't mean you should immediately try a mogul-filled "Most Difficult" run. For the experience to be productive, there should be a gradual progression of difficulty. If you step too far over the line of your perceived ability, you'll end up being frustrated, or, worse, paralyzed with fear.

Provided the run you choose isn't congested with other skiers, you can begin exploring slope steepness on an "Easiest" slope. The best time to do this is early in the morning, right after the lifts have opened. After you've had a warm-up run at your usual speed, go down the slope making longer turns, which don't go as far off the fall-line. You should pick a turn radius that gets you going faster, but still allows you to remain in control. Again, make sure you watch out for other skiers as you do this. The idea of skiing at these higher speeds is to develop more dynamic balance in your skiing and to make your movements more spontaneous.

Next, seek out groomed slopes that are just a bit steeper. These will probably be some of the easier "More Difficult" runs on the mountain. Certain runs in this category border on being expert, so if you're not with someone who knows the area well, make sure you ask a ski patrolman how difficult they actually are. Once you've found an appropriate run, try linking together a number of turns (say, 10), maintaining a steady, slow speed. To accomplish this, turn the skis strongly across the fall-line at the end of each curve. As you do this, you'll create sufficient edge angle to produce a "platform" that slows you down and provides a place from which to start the next turn. The more rhythmically you can link one platform to another, the easier you'll be able to maintain good speed control. Once again, the best way to develop turning rhythm is to count out the turns in a steady cadence.

If you're having trouble linking these short turns together on the steep, you may need more work on your pole plant. Remember: placing the pole in the snow comes at the end/beginning of the turn, and primarily involves movement of the wrist. The action of swinging the pole down the slope in the course of the turn helps keep you well-angulated—or in a solid, balanced position over the outside (turning) ski—toward the end of the turn, which is important for maintaining speed on steeper slopes. Possibly the easiest way of getting the timing of these movements is to follow a better skier, and try putting your pole in the same place in the snow that he or she does.

As you ski steeper slopes, pole placement becomes more and more critical. Notice that the hands remain relatively level and that the wrist's cocking motion brings the pole tip forward.

A

B

C

After you're able to maintain good speed control on this slope with the original radius, try making a series of larger turns at the same speed. You can do this simply by slowing the cadence of your count. Notice that the skis end up at approximately the same angle across the hill, but the pressure you feel in the soles of your feet is softer and lasts longer. Rather than making a rapid hit on the edges at the end of the skid, as in the short turn, you have time to savor the pressure for a while. Long turns provide an opportunity for more rest between turns, and knowing how to conserve energy is something worth having in your bag of tricks.

Obviously there are more than two turn radii, so you should experiment thoroughly with different cadences to create different turn shapes. Become aware of how the speed of flexing the legs at the finish of the turn, and then extending the legs as you start up the next turn, changes with different radii.

Ice

Despite the excellent grooming done by most areas, at some point you will find yourself skiing on hard-packed snow or even ice. These conditions create a genuine challenge, but they can be handled easily with the right tools. First, it helps to keep your skis sharpened. Rental skis are usually sharp, but if you own your own, make sure you maintain them regularly, as discussed in the section on "Ski Tuning." Still, even if your skis are sharp, don't expect them to feel as stable as they do on soft snow. Ice allows for little or no edge penetration, so you will not have as good a platform at the end of a turn. If you accept this and don't panic, your skiing will still be fun.

One nice thing about ice is that skis turn more easily on it than on snow. Try to take this lack of turning resistance into account as you guide the skis. If you use the same amount of rotary power you used on packed snow, you'll turn your skis right back up the hill. Keep that in mind and temper the amount of muscular effort you use to point the skis in the direction you want to go.

It is very important to keep your weight on the outside ski. Leaning in and getting on the inside ski doesn't work well, but it is difficult to make the mental commitment to stay in an angular relationship with the turning ski on an icy slope. The natural reaction is to lean into the hill instead of leaning into the ski. The problem with leaning in is that it puts your weight on the inside ski and you can't catch your balance if the ski should slip. Since slipping is a fact of life on hard snow and ice, you must learn to keep your weight on the outside ski in this condition.

There are basically two schools of thought concerning how best to apply pressure to the outside ski in icy conditions. The classic method is to get on and off the turning ski as fast as possible. That requires a quick weight transfer from ski to ski and a rhythmic turning cadence. The other option is to apply pressure to the turning ski as smoothly as possible. To do this, try to settle onto your outside ski with a pressure you might associate with the sound yaaaaaah, rather than YAH as in the first option. This slower cadence will produce longer turns. Which method is preferable? It depends. The quick-hit-and-off method is very dependable, provided you can maintain rhythm from one turn to another. It's the more aggressive way to ski ice, but it requires proportionally greater muscular effort. The longer-turn approach, with a softer pressuring of the skis, allows you to rest more between turns. With either method, you will end up skidding—there's no way not to—so accept that and maintain your balance by staying over the downhill (outside) ski. The skills you learned at the beginning of this chapter on sideslipping are especially applicable to ice skiing.

Bumps

As discussed in Chapter One, moguls are piles of packed snow formed by turns being made in the same general location. Even at areas that do an excellent grooming job, bumps develop on ski runs by late afternoon each day. Many people will try anything to avoid bumpy slopes, saying that they can't ski them. This is unfortunate, because moguls actually make skiing much easier.

It is important to understand that a mogul is a convex surface on the plane of the ski slope. As you go over one, your skis lighten naturally just as a car does when it crests a rise in the road surface. When you take advantage of this so-called "terrain unweighting" it is much easier to make the skis turn. Bumps also reduce the amount of contact your skis have with the snow. If you stand directly on top of a bump, it is easy to see this teeter-totter effect.

The teeter-totter effect makes turning on bumps easy. Since only the middle of the ski is in contact with the snow, you just pivot the skis in the direction you want to go.

The key to basic bump skiing is to slow down before you reach the crest of the bump. If you are not in control when you get there, you'll end up being launched by the mogul. To slow down, you must finish the previous turn strongly as you come into the front side of the bump, similar to the way you turned to make a hockey stop. The edging and rotary skills you learned while skiing the steep will come in handy here.

After you've created a solid platform and slowed yourself down, making a bump turn is easy. Plant your downhill pole in the snow for balance, and tip and turn the skis at the crest of the bump in the direction you want to go. An important point to remember as you make the turn is to be certain you're in the process of transferring your weight to the new outside ski as you approach the top of the bump. For more information on bump skiing, see "Aerial Turns" and "Ski-Snow Contact" in the following chapter.

Powder Snow

Powder snow provides one of the true joys of skiing, but at the intermediate level it often causes serious problems. The difficulties associated with this snow condition are legitimate when the new snow is windblown, heavy, or more than a foot deep. In these instances there is substantial resistance to turning, and you're better off staying on the packed runs if at all possible. Many times, however, the problems one has with powder snow are mainly psychological: not being able to see the skis. Remember that what you want to do as you ski is feel the skis, not look at them. Keeping that in mind and looking down the slope helps makes powder skiing much easier.

Another important skill necessary in skiing powder snow is unweighting. Unlike skiing moguls, where the convex surface of the bump lightens your skis, in powder you have to do the job yourself by making a pronounced extension of your legs to start the turn. Since the forces that build up at the end of a turn cause your legs to be flexed anyway, this extending movement is a very natural one. By linking one turn to another, you begin to get a feel for the beautiful floating sensation that makes powder snow so positively addictive.

If you feel tentative as you ski powder, try making a few turns into the hill. The technique required is similar to that for hockey stops from a traverse, which we discussed at the beginning of this chapter. If the snow is really deep, flex down low as you're going across the hill, then extend your legs, while simultaneously turning your skis into the hill. Gradually steepen the traverse and notice how much easier it is to make the turn when you are going a bit faster. Even though there is some additional resistance, the skis will come around if you are patient. Don't fall into the trap of losing your balance by abruptly forcing the skis around the turn.

A popular misconception skiers have, and one that gets them out of balance in powder snow, is that they must lean back to prevent their ski tips from submarining beneath the surface. Even in very deep snow this is not the case. Sitting back causes severe muscle fatigue and limits the effective use of rotator muscles in the legs to make turns. The goal in powder snow is to maintain a balanced stance in the middle of the skis. Since deeper snow creates a certain resistance to sliding, it may appear that more proficient skiers are leaning back, but what they are actually doing is keeping a centered fore/aft balance. This is especially misleading in very deep snow, where the skier is actually balancing on a platform of snow whose pitch is shallower than the true pitch of the slope.

Other Conditions to Watch For

Between the extremes of fresh, unpacked powder and hard, granular ice lies a wide spectrum of snow conditions that everyone eventually encounters in the course of his skiing career. Some pose special problems for even the most tested skier, and a few, such as porous, rotten, end-of-season snow, can be outright dangerous. What follows is a list of additional snow conditions to watch for, and a few tips on how to deal with each.

- *Fresh powder into semipacked powder.* Sometimes after a fall of fresh powder, you'll leave the pristine conditions in which you've been skiing and find yourself skiing on powder that has been broken up by others' skis. Normally, the moment your skis hit that semipacked condition, they accelerate, and if you're not prepared for the transition, you can fall. It's important, therefore, to look ahead, keep your hands ahead of you, and maintain balance on the center of your skis.
- *Icy spots between bumps.* If you're not careful in this condition, your skis can spin out from under you as you try to turn. To negotiate icy spots between bumps (moguls), slow down, look ahead, and either ski wide of the icy spots or take shorter turns, and then be prepared for your skis to slow down and for your edges to feel as if they are gripping when they return to the less icy snow. In general, taking shorter turns and applying less rotary power to them will carry you through the iciest bump field.
- *Cut-up snow.* In this condition (fresh snow that has been skied on but not rolled), the snow is unpacked and disconcerting to ski on because

it lacks powder snow's consistency. To negotiate it, *be strong on your skis,* actively guiding them through the turn shapes you're trying to produce.

- *Windpacked snow.* As the term implies, windpack is snow that has been compressed by high winds and is slabby (it can be lifted in flat wide chunks) and difficult to turn in. When skiing windpack, the temptation is to slow down, but a slightly higher speed is very helpful. Going faster, combined with applying *more* rotary power, will allow you to cut through the windpack's crust. Equally important: be sure to make *pronounced edge changing movements*—that is, be decisive about tipping your skis onto their new inside edges as you initiate each turn to avoid the possibility of catching your outside edges.

- *Cat tracks.* Snow-grooming machines, sometimes called snow cats, leave tread tracks in the snow, and if conditions turn granular or icy, these tracks can be treacherous to ski on—your skis can either vibrate out of control, or a ski's tip or edge can catch in the track, causing a nasty fall. *Never ski fast over cat tracks;* look ahead, spot them well in advance, and ski over them slowly.

- *Spring conditions.* Spring skiing can be a joyous experience: warm, sunny days, fewer people on trails and lifts, and excellent, albeit different, snow conditions. You probably won't be skiing powder in the spring (unless you ski in the West, where late-season snow squalls are commonplace), but you will be skiing on an equally delightful snow that most experienced skiers call *corn.* In shape and texture, corn snow resembles loose, hard corn kernals, and its peculiar characteristics are the result of repeated melting and freezing: the snowflakes lose their pointiness, consolidate, melt somewhat during the day, and refreeze at night so that they are like pellets when they melt the next day.

Because of the way snow freezes and thaws in the spring, a day of spring skiing is one of ever-changing snow conditions, influenced both by temperature and sun angle. In the morning, the snow is hard and icy, and unless you feel comfortable on it, you probably shouldn't plan on an early start. By ten or eleven o'clock, however, as the angle of the sun changes, the temperature rises and melting occurs, the iciness disappears, and the snow "corns up." If you decide to do some corn-snow skiing, plan on skiing slower and work at developing a smooth, deliberate turning rhythm, staying centered on your skis, or even slightly back on them if the snow becomes sticky, and apply a bit more rotary power to your turns to counteract the snow's heaviness. *Be extra-careful when skiing bumps in the spring.* The snow can become soft and mushy in the troughs, owing to meltage, and you can bury your ski tips into the side of the mogul before you know it.

Usually, near the bottom of the hill, the snow is thick and mushy, and again you should be prepared for your skis to slow abruptly in it. To counteract undue deceleration, consider *lengthening* your turns or running straight if the terrain allows it; that way, you'll maintain your momentum and not have to walk to the bottom.

If the day warms up too much, the snow can turn from corn to "mashed potatoes"—an apt term for that snow and a terrible condition to ski in. Your skis feel as if they're pushing through mucilage. As you hit mashed-potato conditions, *slow way down,* make short, forceful turns, and, once you reach the bottom of the slope, take off your skis, go out on the deck of the ski lodge and bag a few rays. Mashed-potato snow is no fun to ski in; indeed, going back for more mashed-potato skiing is an invitation to possible injury.

Even more caution should be applied if you have to ski old, porous, "rotten" snow; you can bury a tip in it and fall before you know what's happening. At the first sign of rotten conditions, get off the slope; you can break a leg in the stuff, or cut yourself against its coral-like edges.

As the spring day wears on and the sun starts to drop, the temperature does, too, and the snow rehardens. Where an hour earlier you had to push your skis forcefully through the heavy corn, now conditions are turning icy again, and your skis move quicker. Time to shorten your turns, cut back on your rotary power, and concentrate on staying balanced over the center of your skis; you're skiing on ice again, and another great day of corn skiing is over.

As you can see, not every day will be one of champagne snow or groomed packed powder, but there's still plenty to enjoy, even when conditions become marginal. Remember the following points when skiing in less-than-perfect snow conditions, and if you still feel uncomfortable in them, talk to a ski instructor about how to handle them best.

1. Maintain balance on the center of your skis.
2. Keep your hands ahead of you.
3. If uncertain of the snow condition, slow down.
4. Look forward, not down; *anticipate* changing conditions.
5. Regulate the amount of rotary power you use when turning, based on the snow's turning resistance. That is, in icy conditions, use less rotary power; in heavy snow conditions, use more.

Once you feel comfortable as an intermediate skier, skiing powder is an experience not to be missed.

6. Make shorter turns in difficult conditions so that you can get on and off the turning ski quickly.

7. Use common sense. If snow conditions are wretched, don't court injury by continuing to ski.

In any of these conditions, it helps to apply the basics: proper edge change, turn radius, balance. These fundamentals can help you through the iciest Eastern bump field, or the thickest "Sierra cement."

CONCLUSION

As you seek out the mileage necessary to learn the skills discussed in this chapter, be very aware of trail markings, particularly if you're trying unfamiliar ski areas. Know that a blue-square, "More Difficult" slope at Buck Hill, Minnesota, has a degree of difficulty different from that of a slope with the same marking at Aspen, Colorado. Any time you're skiing at a major resort, move to the more difficult trails with caution. If you don't, you might find yourself in way over your head. Another thing: take a lesson the first day you're at a new area. A lesson will give you a guided tour of the slopes as well as supply the feedback that is so important to make your practice perfect.

Advanced Skiing

Making the jump from the intermediate to the expert level of skiing isn't easy. It takes mileage and many hours of practice to hone your skills to handle any terrain or snow condition that a mountain presents. Surprisingly, though, you can reach expert levels of skiing even if you're not a gifted, "natural" athlete. All it takes is commitment, time, and lots of energy.

Through the years many people have heeded this call to put in the miles necessary to become expert skiers. They go skiing two or three nights each week and religiously travel to major ski resorts every weekend during the winter. They read ski magazines, train for skiing in the off-season, and talk up the sport at every opportunity. And when the cravings get too great, some quit their jobs and find employment in resort towns so they can get out on the mountain every day. Though the "ski bum" of days past is a vanishing breed, urban transplants still come to the mountains each year lured by the promise of expert skiing.

The allure of expert skiing is the freedom it provides. The feeling is certainly present at all levels of the sport but doesn't fully manifest itself until you can genuinely make turns anywhere on the mountain. Regardless of snow conditions, ter-

125

The advanced skier is able to handle any terrain or snow conditions that a mountain presents.

rain, or the task at hand, the expert skier moves in harmony with the surroundings. His movements are fluid and graceful thanks to thousands of skiing solutions stored in his muscles' memories. Indeed, the expert's movements are so thoroughly ingrained that many are no longer conscious—actions have become pure reflex.

Just as there are many levels of proficiency in the intermediate realm of skiing, so too is there a hierarchy of expert skiing. How far you rise on the ladder is dependent, first, upon the controllable aspects of skiing: physical conditioning, sound fundamentals, and, to a lesser extent, the quality of the equipment you are using. Thereafter, to become a world-class racer or a truly extraordinary expert skier usually requires an extra helping of athletic ability and a long-term involvement with the sport dating back to childhood. Still, anyone can become an expert with properly directed practice. This chapter provides some guidelines, many of which are also applicable to intermediate skiers.

EXERCISES AND GAMES FOR ADVANCED SKIERS: AN OVERVIEW

As a premise underlying what follows, remember that skiing is a very simple activity. You have to tip the ski on edge, put your weight on it, and supply some rotary power to make the skis come around the turn. With that in mind, try to perform the following tasks as efficiently as possible. The goal is to make only those movements which help you control the skis. While this goal applies at all levels, you must genuinely master movement efficiency to become an expert. At this level there can be no wasted motion. You will note that several of the following exercises and games have been discussed previously. The difference in the way they are performed now is the level of dexterity with which you guide the skis. To become an expert, you must think of the skis as an extension of your mind—in other words, as an appendage you control—just as naturally as you do your hand as it turns the pages of this book. When you gain this control, the mountain becomes a true playground, a place where you dance with the rhythm it presents on any day.

The following list of exercises and games does not purport to be complete. Advanced skiing has so many aspects that it could easily be the subject of an entire book by itself. What follows are only a few of my favorite exercises for advanced skiing. Consider them only a starting point.

Lead/follow
When playing lead/follow, try to keep your skis in exactly the same track as the person you're following. You do that by turning *where* the person does, not *when* she does.

PARTNER EXERCISES

Lead/Follow

Following another skier, ideally one who is better than you, is one of the best ways to develop rhythm and spontaneous movements. You get the most out of this experience by trying to put your skis directly in the track scribed by the lead skier's turns. Play, at first, with turns of a constant radius and cadence. Remember that you are trying to turn where, not when, the lead skier did. A good trick for achieving this is to try to plant your pole in exactly the same spot that the lead skier put his or hers.

Once you have experimented with various constant-radius turns, ask the lead skier to turn in an arrhythmic fashion, that is, make a couple of short turns, some medium ones, turns across the hill, etc. The person in front should deliberately ski a lead that is difficult to follow, so that you have to really work and stay attentive to keep your skis in the track. Where the rhythmic lead helped your visual targeting and helped ingrain solid movement patterns, this arrhythmic lead helps make you more versatile and spontaneous.

Another way to work on spontaneity and versatility is to play a game of "Simon Says." The person in front should mix up the turn initiations and you should copy what he or she does. You could start out with a few parallel initiations, do several skating or stem steps, and even throw in a few wedge turns if the terrain is appropriate. The goal again is to increase your overall skill level by challenging your ability to start turns in different ways.

Name That Run

This game involves two or more people, standing at the top of a ski run. Pick out a finishing point—say, 100 yards down the mountain—and try to predict how many turns it will take you to get there. If you said it would take eight turns, the goal is to make those turns at a constant speed and radius. You'll find that this game helps you learn to shape a turn to accomplish a given task. Very often, "name that run" turns into a fool's game of how few turns you can make between point "A" and point "B." Don't play it that way. It is much more challenging—and much safer—to make a sane number of graceful curves between two points than it is to cannonball the run to impress your friends.

Max Turns Challenge

This is a great exercise for a cold day or for a ski area that isn't particularly challenging. As in the previous game, you determine starting and ending points, but the distance required is much shorter—say, 25 yards. The goal is to try to make as many turns as possible between the two points. Any sort of turn will work, but short-radius parallel turns, or stem steps, are probably the best. As you do them, count each complete turn that you make. The winner is the person who can make the most turns between the two points.

With max turns, you are trying to make as many turns as possible in a given distance, but be sure to maintain good quality as you do them. It is far better to make 10 good turns in that 25 yards than to make 15 sloppy ones. Begin with quality, then gradually increase the quantity. By performing this task, you can make significant improvements in your quickness from ski to ski. "Quick feet" are essential for skiing situations like bumps, narrow trails, and the steeps.

Synchronized Skiing

Synchronized skiing is a variation on the lead/follow theme. Instead of trying to guide your skis through the exact track of the lead skier, you turn at the same time as the person in front of you, mirroring your partner's movements. After

Synchronized Skiing

Another excellent way to add rhythm and spontaneity to your skiing is via synchronized skiing. Mirror the movements of the lead skier as closely as possible.

A

B

C

D

you've tried this for a while, you'll notice that, to ski in synch successfully, you must feel the lead skier's rhythm and anticipate his or her turns. Waiting until you see the lead skier start turning will leave you behind and out of sync.

Skating Races

Skating races are another game you play over a predetermined distance. You and your partner should point yourself straight down the hill. Ideally, a third person gives the signal. When that person says, "Go!" you and your partner skate as fast as you can straight down the hill. Since you obviously pick up a considerable amount of speed doing this, it is important that the slope be uncrowded, well-groomed, and not too steep. Make sure there is a good runout, and decide beforehand which direction you'll turn to come to a stop—if the

A

Skating races
These are a fun way to warm up and they help develop many skills involved in upper-level skiing.

B

person on the left turns to the right, and the other to the left, in a close race a collision is nearly inevitable.

There are a number of benefits from this seemingly crazy exercise. It develops better edge engagement, better transfer of weight from ski to ski, and more efficient movements. You can tell how good a skier someone is by how well the person skates on skis, and even if you don't have a partner, working on skating straight down the hill is a productive exercise. Be careful to make a definite commitment to the ski you are skating onto. If you do not push off directly onto that ski, it is very easy to get hung up between the skis and do a split.

MOUNTAIN EXPERIENCE CLASSES

Another way to improve your skiing is a "mountain experience" type of class. Originally started at Snowbird, Utah, these ski school classes are now available at major ski areas around the country. They usually take a limited number of students, and their emphasis is on teaching people to ski all the terrain and snow conditions the mountain has to offer.

A typical mountain experience lesson is four hours long, and within that period will take you on as many runs as possible. The teacher will give you tips on how to improve your skiing, but the emphasis is on mileage. This is a useful option on crowded weekend days, as the classes usually have lift-line cutting privileges, and, because the person in charge of the class is selected by the ski school director on the basis of knowledge of the ski area, mountain experience lessons are a great way to ski "secret spots" that you wouldn't ordinarily learn of.

INDIVIDUAL EXERCISES

Leapers

"Leapers" are critical exercise for improving your balance and range of motion on skis. To learn how to do them, begin by making some short-radius turns where you get the skis completely off the snow at the beginning of the turn. You lift the skis by forcefully straightening (extending) your legs at the end of the previous turn. Once this movement has gotten the skis off the snow, pivot them in the direction you want to go. Land on a flat ski (or slightly on the inside edges) somewhere around the fall-line, and complete the turn with a solid

A

Leapers

Leapers are a great way to get the feel for the flexing and extending motions the legs must perform in all turns.

B

C

D

E

After you've gotten the hang of doing this "full pivot" type of short turn, try some larger-radius turns where you still hop the skis off the snow at the initiation. These turns are called leapers, and to do them smoothly, you have to try to keep your flexing and extending movements as continuous as possible.

After doing a number of leapers, try making some turns where the up-and-down motion is less dramatic. Try to maintain movements that are similar but not so powerful that the skis are pulled off the snow. The flexing and extending movements you learned in the leapers should make the turns link together more easily. You'll notice that there is a definite difference between the intensity of rotary power in short-radius turns and in longer ones. Why? In short turns you need to guide, or point, the skis to get them going in the direction you want to go. In longer turns, the pointing action is much more subtle since the radius of the turn is elongated.

The flexion and extension you learn from leapers is important for a number of reasons. From a physiological standpoint, pumping the legs this way helps provide blood and oxygen to the muscles, which in turn allows you to ski longer, with less fatigue. Another important benefit is that these movements are essential for you to ski powder and junk snow effectively. Being able to un-weight your skis becomes increasingly important as turning resistance develops in deeper snow conditions.

Aerial Turns

Similar to the skills you learned from leapers are those involved in aerial turns. Besides looking flashy, aerial turns are essential for skiing moguls effectively. When you're skiing a bump field at higher speeds, you need to be able to get off the ground on occasion to find a better place to turn. Aerial turns allow that. Besides, getting in the air is one of the fun aspects of skiing.

Begin by practicing on a small bump, and pick a slope that isn't too intimidating. Aim for the very top of the mogul in a tall stance, and keep your legs loose enough that the bump's convex surface flexes your legs slightly. The next step is to extend your legs the moment you reach the crest so that you are propelled into the air. Once you're in the air, delicately turn your skis down the hill. It is important to be gentle, because if you rotate your legs too strongly, you'll end up landing sideways and crash instantly. The idea is to turn the skis just enough that they land at, or slightly before, the fall-line.

One thing that helps improve aerial turns, and bump skiing in general, is

Aerial Turns

A

B

To do an aerial turn off a mogul, aim for the top of the mogul in a tall stance, keeping your legs slightly loose (A).

At the moment you reach the crest, extend your legs to propel yourself into the air (B).

C

Once you're in the air, delicately turn your skis down the hill (C,D). Don't over-rotate; you'll land sideways and crash.

D

With your legs extended fully, they can flex more easily to absorb the shock of impact (E). Try to get snow contact as quickly as possible with the outside leg.

E

to *think about reestablishing snow contact as quickly as possible with the outside* 135
leg. Think of this as reaching for the snow with the new turning ski. As you
go over the bump, you can accomplish this reaching by trying to touch down
softly on the inside edge of the outside ski. This gives you immediate control
of the new turning ski and puts you in a strong position of balance for the new
turn.

After you've done a few aerial turns individually, find a gentle mogul field
and try doing an aerial on every turn. You'll look like a rabbit hopping down
the mountain, but this exercise dramatically improves your stance on the skis
and ingrains the ability to stay in control while taking air. Getting off the
ground on occasion is inevitable in advanced skiing, so it is good to practice
it in a controlled situation.

Ski-Snow Contact

At the other end of the spectrum from aerial turns is trying to maintain
ski-snow contact in the moguls. This is very important since it is the primary
method you use in day-to-day bump skiing. The key ingredients for keeping the
skis on the snow in varied terrain are *absorption* and *line judgment.*

Absorbing the terrain involves what Georges Joubert originally described
as "avalement." The word literally means "to swallow," and the technique is
accomplished by using the legs as shock absorbers. As the bump begins to push
up on the legs, you retract them, while simultaneously contracting your stomach muscles. Tightening the abdomen is critical because it helps keep the upper
body in balance. If you don't do this, all your weight will end up on the tails
of the skis as you pull up your legs to swallow the mogul. Equally important
is extending your legs as you pass over the top of the mogul, since you have
to put the "landing gear" back down to accomplish your goal of ski-snow
contact.

To learn the fundamentals of avalement, traverse across a series of fairly
large moguls and try to keep the skis snaking along the surface of the snow.
To do this, you have to retract/contract, then extend, on each bump. After
several tries, this pumping action of the legs should start to feel quite natural.

To put terrain absorption into use while turning, go to the top of a "more
difficult" mogul slope and look carefully at the surface. Although at first glance
it looks like a crazy quilt, there's usually a certain order to a mogul field. Notice
that the high points are separated by deep depressions. These are called *troughs.*
In trying to maintain ski-snow contact, plan to ski this "trough line."

It is very important to keep yourself going down the hill when skiing
bumps. The trough line tries to bring you there, but it's easy to lose confidence

A

B

C

Skiing the Bumps: Avalement

When skiing bumps, remember: Retract, contract, extend. Here, as the bump begins to push up on the skier's legs (A), he retracts them (B) and simultaneously contracts his stomach muscles to keep his upper body balanced. He then pivots his skis in the direction he wants to go (C) and extends his legs to re-establish ski-snow contact as quickly as possible (D,E).

D

E

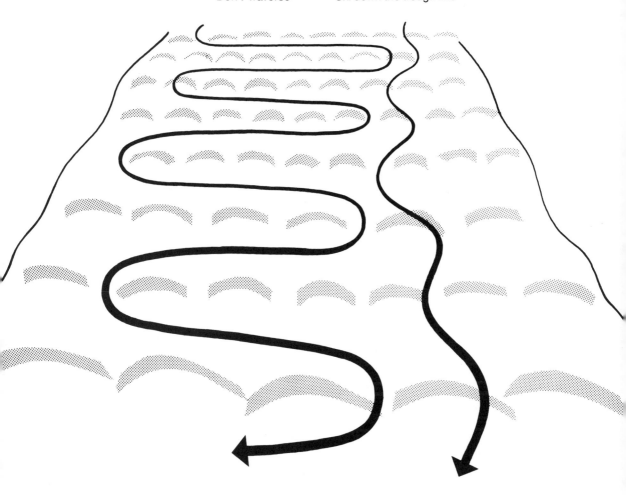

WRONG:
Don't traverse

RIGHT:
Ski down the trough line

When skiing bumps, ski *down* the mountain in the trough line. Don't traverse.

Skiing the Bumps:
Moving Down the Fall-Line

It is all here: The skier retracts his legs, contracts his stomach
muscles, then extends his legs as he makes his way down the
fall-line of the mogul field. Notice, too, how he extends and
plants his left pole as he begins his turn to the left and how he
looks well ahead to stay in the troughs.

and pull out into a traverse. Don't do this. *It is far more tiring to traverse across
moguls than it is to keep yourself turning down the mountain.* Control your
speed with the same method regardless of the terrain—turning your skis across
the hill. You are able to do this in bumps by looking well ahead so that you
can follow the path through the bumps.

Even though this path is a trough, it is not uniformly smooth throughout.
There will be changes in contour as the trough winds its way around the various
moguls. Each time you feel your skis being pushed up by a convex surface,
remember to apply the avalement that you've already practiced: Retract/con-
tract, then extend. Make sure that you plant your ski pole on each turn to aid
in balance and in setting your edges so you have good speed control.

If you get into a situation where the trough you were following terminates, use the aerial turn you learned previously. Rather than absorbing that bump, simply get up in the air and land in another trough line. Obviously it's important to be looking ahead so you can plan for this action and have some idea where you'll want to land. Also remember that you must be ready to absorb as soon as you land.

RECREATIONAL RACING

While helpful at all levels, recreational racing is particularly beneficial for advance skiers. By making turns around gates, you force yourself to turn in definite locations. As you become more proficient at this task, you hone your edging, rotary, and pressure control skills to a level where you can genuinely turn where and when you want to on the open slope. Getting into the gates is one of the easiest and best ways to become an advanced skier.

A race course is basically a series of right and left turns delineated on a ski slope by bamboo or plastic poles. The person who sets the course tries to organize the gates so they flow down the mountain in accordance with the terrain. To set the shape of the turns, the course setter regulates the vertical and horizontal distances of the gates. In working with these variables, abrupt changes of speed or rhythm are generally avoided, even at advanced levels of racing. A well-set course will bring you down the mountain in a very natural sequence of turns.

A   B

On the practice course, a single bamboo pole before a gate is called a "helper pole," and it denotes the spot on the rise line where you should start your turn (A). By starting the turn at the helper pole, you can finish the turn at the gate (B).

Line judgment is the most fundamental thing you need to know when skiing a race course. It is difficult, because the path you take through the poles violates something you've known since childhood—that the shortest (fastest) way to move between two points is in a straight line. While this is certainly true when you are walking between point "a" and "b," it is not true in ski racing. If you go directly at the gate, then try to turn, you'll end up skidding sideways and won't be able to make a smooth turn around the next gate.

To prevent this from happening, *think of the gate as the end, rather than the beginning, of the turn.* By the time you go past the gate, your direction change should be virtually complete and you should be preparing for the next turn. One of the easiest ways to ensure proper line in the gates is to imagine that there is a vertical line running uphill from the pole. The first person I heard talk about this was Warren Witherell, former headmaster of the Burke Mountain Racing Academy in northern Vermont. Witherell calls this imaginary line the "rise line." The further the horizontal distance of the next gate, the higher you should start your turn on the rise line. Conversely, the shorter the horizontal distance, the lower you can start your turn on the rise line. If you are working in a race class at a ski area, helper poles will probably be placed above the gates so you know where to start the turns.

Invariably, you will end up being too low for a gate in spite of your best efforts to ski the proper line. There are two ways to handle this problem. If you are just slightly low, stay on the turn a bit longer and make the Diverging Step turn discussed in Chapter Five. With a solid edge to push off from, you can easily regain several feet by making a strong lateral movement to the ski you are stepping onto. If you've gotten really low, don't try to make it all up in one turn. Gradually gain height with a successive number of step turns and you will eventually find yourself back on track. In either case, after the run, try to determine what happened that caused you to get off line. You may have just misjudged the severity of the turns that the course setter delineated, or you may have had some technical problem that prevented you from making the desired turn. If you can't figure it out for yourself, ask someone who observed your run, so that you can avoid repeating the mistake.

To ski a good line in the gates, it is important always to inspect the course before running it. Visualize where you will exit each gate of the course, and know how far up on the rise line you'll need to be to end up there. If the course goes over dropoffs, pick a point on the horizon that will help you line up for the gate that you can't see above the knoll. Prior planning is very important for doing your best in the gates.

If you are racing against the clock, it is also important to know about starting and finishing. Many skiers lose time by improper technique at the beginning or end of the course. Your time in a race course is computed by a clock that is activated when your legs brush a nylon wand at the start and is turned off by a photoelectric cell at the finish. Since your lower legs trip the starting wand, it is important to get as much of your body moving down the hill before you actually start the timer. The easiest way to do this is simply to lean forward off the start ramp. Jump starts, which involve kicking the legs backwards as the upper body vaults forward with the help of the ski poles, supply much more initial forward momentum but are quite a bit more difficult. Whichever starting technique you choose, it is important to have someone giving you feedback as you practice. Make sure that you are not kicking your foot forward as you go out of the start, as this will start the clock before you get going down the course.

Another aspect of starting is to plan where you want to go with this push down the mountain. You have to look carefully at the first gate and determine where you want to be on the rise line of that pole. It is very easy to go too straight at the first gate and end up being late for the first couple of turns. The

Racing Starts: The Leaning Start

A　　　　　　　　　　B　　　　　　　　　　C

Beginning racers should simply lean forward while simultaneously pulling forward on the ski poles with both arms (A,B). The goal is to get as much of your body as possible moving down the hill before your legs trip the starting wand (C,D).

Racing Starts: The Jump Start

A　　　　　　　　　　B　　　　　　　　　　C

For more momentum in your race starts, lean forward as usual (A), but add a backward kick with one leg (B,C,D). Note the near-egg crouch the racer assumes upon take-off (E,F) to minimize wind resistance.

D

D

E

F

opposite problem is going too high above the first gate and traveling extra distance. Poor judgment either way will add seconds to your overall time.

For recreational as well as very advanced racers, the goal in approaching the finish is not so much to gain time as not to lose time. One basic mistake people make at the end of a race course is to turn through the finish line. While you are inspecting the course, try to see the shortest possible distance between the last gate and the imaginary line of the photoelectric cell that stops the clock. You want to keep your skis gliding as flat as possible on the snow from the last gate. This simple rule is much more effective and safe than the current rage of trying to jet your skis out in front of you by sitting back on the tails at the finish.

There are many avenues for the pursuit of recreational racing. NASTAR, as previously mentioned, is the National Standard Race. Each time you race you receive a handicap, based on the pacesetter's time for the course. Since the pacesetter had to compete nationally to receive his own handicap, this system allows you to compare your progress to that of skiers around the country. Depending on your age, the handicap you receive will qualify you for bronze, silver, or gold medals from NASTAR. National winners in the various age categories are also eligible for an all-expense paid trip to the U.S. Championships, held at a different ski area each spring.

You can also get time in the gates by participating in racing ski weeks held at various ski areas. These five-day packages, which typically provide lodging, lift tickets, and daily coaching, are a satisfying way to learn more about racing. Time is spent on the technical and tactical aspects of ski racing, and there is usually a fun race among the participants at the conclusion. If you don't have time to commit to an entire week, most ski schools or mountain race departments offer group race lessons on a daily basis. While less extensive than an entire week of race training, they are an easy way to pick up the fundamentals.

A variation of an individual or week-long race class is the summer race camp. These programs, offered for children and adults, provide an intensive race training environment. They are offered at year-round ski areas in North America and in more exotic camps in the Southern Hemisphere, primarily in New Zealand and Chile. At these camps you eat, sleep, and breathe ski racing, and after a week in one, you should have made a significant improvement in your gate-running skills. To find out what's available in the summer, check the spring issues of the major skiing magazines.

Another way to test your ability is to participate in "Masters Racing," the ultimate competition available for adult racers. This series of ski races runs all winter long and divides participants into various age categories. You can attend slalom races (tight turns with an average speed of perhaps 25 miles per hour),

Racing helps make your progress in skiing what it should be: fun.

giant slalom races (a stretched-out slalom with average speeds of about 35 miles per hour), or even downhill races (long turns with speeds approaching 60 miles per hour). You can get information about Masters Series racing through the race department or ski school at your local area.

CONCLUSION

However you apply the various exercises and games discussed in this chapter, I reiterate, *you must make a point of getting feedback on your progress.* Many people stop looking for instruction as they enter the realm of advanced skiing. That's a mistake. At any level of the sport, the amount of time you spend doing it is only as good as the quality of the movements you are practicing. By regularly checking in with a qualified professional, you will receive the direction and guidance necessary to become an expert skier.

7

Conditioning and Ski-Specific Exercises

Physical fitness is especially important in skiing. Although skis are designed for easy turning, muscular effort is definitely required to make them turn. The mountain you ski on also places physical demands on your body since the contour of the slope is constantly changing. Bumps, dips, and rolls force your entire body—especially your legs—to act as shock absorbers to maintain your balance over this undulating terrain. If you are not in shape to ski, then by the end of a day on the slopes you'll feel like a limp noodle.

Two things have been proven repeatedly concerning the relationship of physical fitness to skiing:

1) *People who are in shape to ski learn much faster.* There's no comparison between the rate of learning of someone who's in good physical condition and of someone who's not. For very good skiers, often the only way to improve is by getting stronger physically.

2) *Conditioning can dramatically reduce your chances of a ski accident or injury.* By developing certain muscle groups, you can protect the various joints and ligaments in your body. In addition, muscles that are less tired will respond more quickly and allow you to ski your way out of trouble, should trouble occur.

147

Ski-specific exercise, such as biking, should be part of any skier's off-season fitness program.

Ski-specific physical conditioning differs from other exercise programs only in emphasis. The basics are still:

1) *muscle overload* (doing sufficient work to stimulate changes in the muscle fibers)

2) *stretching* (maintaining muscle elasticity and joint flexibility as these changes take place)

3) *nutrition* (ingesting the proper fuel for the muscles to function and rebuild themselves)

4) *rest* (getting adequate sleep to allow the body to rejuvenate itself)

Like other exercise, the program results in improved cardiovascular fitness, greater strength, and flexibility. But to make the time spent most effective for improved skiing performance, you have to direct your program to the specific needs of alpine skiing.

Although the physical fitness boom has certainly taken hold in this country, it is much easier to talk about doing drills and exercises for skiing than to do them. The work outlined in this chapter is recommended especially (though not entirely) for the off-season and is not always fun. Rainy days and tired muscles are often a reality, and there will be many times when you just don't feel like working out. Unfortunately, if you're planning on getting in shape, you have to go out anyway. There is no way to get in good physical condition without a year-round, regular program of exercise. Your motivation in this regard is totally self-centered. You will feel better, look better, be less prone to injury, and, most of all, you will ski better. There is some pain involved, but, believe me, it is worth the effort.

If you are not on some sort of conditioning program already, you should have a complete physical examination by a doctor. This is especially true if you are over the age of 35 or have a history of heart problems in your family. If you are in either or both of these categories, don't try to apply any of the suggestions in this chapter without first seeing a physician.

DEVELOP A CONDITIONING BASE

To train for skiing, the first thing you must do is build up an *aerobic base.* As in other sports, this system is the foundation for all other conditioning. The aerobic system refers to muscle-energy production with the aid of oxygen. In technical terms, carbohydrates (muscle glycogen) and fat are oxidized to produce the fuel that powers your muscles to contract. When you have been conditioning this system, your body has a greater capacity to gather, move, and use oxygen. Such efficiency is important for skiing because much of the energy the sport requires can be produced by the aerobic system. Aerobic exercise is characterized by *longer workouts at moderate levels of intensity.* The easiest way to determine whether you are achieving the proper level of intensity is to monitor your heart rate. A simple way of checking your pulse is to count the number of beats that occur in 10 seconds, and multiply by six. Many people will use the carotid artery in the neck to check their pulse, but exercise physiologists have discovered that this may lead to an inaccurate measurement. Furthermore, if you press too hard on this artery, you run the risk of reducing blood flow to the brain. It is preferable to check your pulse at the wrist.

For aerobic conditioning to occur, you have to be working at 70 to 85 percent of your maximum heart rate. Although a stress test can determine your exact maximum, a rough estimate can be determined by subtracting your age from 220. Therefore, a 30-year-old person has a maximum heart rate of 190 beats per minute. For this person to achieve effective aerobic training would require a heart rate during exercise of 133 to 161 beats per minute. As your conditioning improves your heart rate will return to normal very quickly, so it is important to check your pulse immediately after the exercise has stopped. Another way to gauge aerobic exercise is to determine whether you can carry on a conversation while you're doing it. If you're out of breath and can't speak, you are beyond your aerobic threshold.

There are numerous ways to train with the aerobic system. Easy running, hiking, biking, swimming, and floor exercise tapes are a few of the options available to you. Whichever you choose, be sure to keep your heart rate within the preceding guidelines. At first you'll probably have to monitor your pulse quite closely, but after a time you'll develop a feel for your own aerobic minimums and maximums.

For any significant improvement in your conditioning to occur, you need to do this sort of exercise for a minimum of 15 minutes a day, at least three times each week. It is obviously preferable to devote more time to the process, and unless you are in very poor physical condition you could probably start out at 30 minutes a day, three times a week. Make it interesting by mixing up the training. Alternate between the various forms of aerobic exercise that will be discussed later on in this chapter.

DEVELOP AN ANEROBIC BASE

The other way your muscles produce energy is by the *anerobic system.* As the name implies, this system produces fuel for the muscles without oxygen. Your anerobic system is activated when the intensity of the exercise is so great that adequate oxygen cannot be supplied to the muscles. This system is much less efficient in producing energy to fuel muscular contraction, and it creates lactic acid as a by-product. Lactic acid buildup often results in a slight burning sensation in the muscles and reduces their efficiency.

Skiers must train their anerobic systems because many situations on the slopes require this method of energy production. This is particularly true of beginning skiers who tend to work much harder than they need to, and of advanced skiers who challenge themselves in moguls and powder or by racing. If the anerobic system has not been adequately conditioned, the skier will have some very sore and tired legs by the end of the day.

To achieve anerobic levels of conditioning, you generally *shorten the duration and increase the intensity of any of the suggested methods of aerobic training.* Run, bike, hike, swim, or do floor exercises with much greater output, but for a shorter amount of time. In another contrast to aerobic training, the intensity with which you exercise anerobically should be such that you are out of breath and unable to carry on a conversation.

With anerobic training, we are talking about heart rates of 85 to 100 percent of maximum. For the 30-year-old, that means exercise producing between 161 and 190 beats per minute. When training in this system, it is important to use an interval method of exercise. For example, you might sprint 25 yards, five times, with a one-minute (or longer) rest period between each repetition. For the most effective interval training you should allow your pulse rate to recover to below 125 beats per minute between each pair of intervals.

There is no way around the fact that anerobic training is difficult. It is tiring, sweaty, and it hurts. Beyond the fact that your effort will definitely enhance your skiing performance, the one consolation is that this system can be adopted very quickly. Once you have an adequate aerobic base, you can tune your anerobic system to peak levels of efficiency in a maximum of six weeks. As with aerobic training, you should devote a minimum of 15 minutes a day, three days a week, to anerobic training.

NUTRITION

To fuel your muscles for dryland training and ski your best once winter comes around, you need to be on an athletic diet—the typical American diet will not do. It is too high in fats and protein, and too low in carbohydrates, to power your body for serious physical output. As a guideline, your diet should include

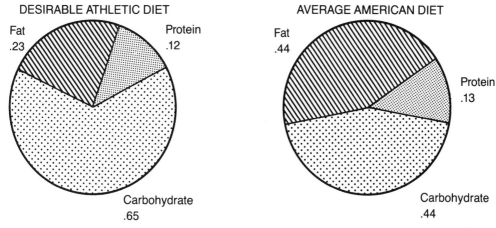

DESIRABLE ATHLETIC DIET

Fat .23

Protein .12

Carbohydrate .65

AVERAGE AMERICAN DIET

Fat .44

Protein .13

Carbohydrate .44

The typical American diet is too high in protein and too low in carbohydrates needed to power the body during strenuous activity.

approximately 20 percent fat, 15 percent protein, and 65 percent carbohydrate for physical training. Although it's difficult to wean yourself from foods high in saturated fats, you can safely reduce the fat intake down to 10 percent and make up the difference with more carbohydrates.

The reasoning behind this suggestion is simple. Muscles are most easily powered by carbohydrates. Although this is a gross oversimplification of exercise physiology, in the aerobic energy producing process, fats and/or carbohydrates are oxidized to create the fuel that allows the muscle to contract. The more intense the work, the more the body relies on carbohydrates in the aerobic process. (Please note that if you are trying to lose weight with exercise, it is best to work at your minimum aerobic threshold so that fat will be used as fuel.) In anerobic exercise, your muscles use fuel from carbohydrates that have been broken down and stored in your muscles.

Carbohydrates do not make you fatter. A potato, for example, which is loaded with carbohydrates, in itself is a non-fattening food. The butter, sour cream, and bacon bits that you put on the potato make it fattening. Likewise, a regular plateful of noodles won't add inches to your waist if you're exercising; smother them in meat sauce and parmesan cheese, however, and they will. Avoid the fatty add-ons and you can eat all the carbohydrates you want.

The best muscle fuel comes from *complex carbohydrates* such as potatoes, whole grain products, and corn. By contrast, you should avoid simple carbohydrates such as those found in candy bars. Refined sugars are a poor source of muscle fuel and tend to dramatically escalate blood sugar levels. In response, the body releases large amounts of insulin to reduce the amount of sugar in the blood. This results in what's been called "the sugar blues," and leaves you more tired than you were in the first place. Recent studies have shown that complex carbohydrates also increase blood sugar levels, but they are still preferable since they supply more vitamins and nutrients than most "junk" foods.

Beyond adequate carbohydrates in your diet, water is the single most important thing for an effective, safe, dryland training program. Fluid loss during exercise can be severe in hot climates. Dehydration robs the muscles of strength and can have dire effects if the body's fluid balance is not maintained. During training you should drink more water than you think you need, as the thirst mechanism of the body often misleads you into believing you've replaced enough water with a single glass. Be aware that you can lose nearly two quarts of water per hour with strenuous exercise in severe heat, and this fluid must be replaced. Although you don't lose fluid as fast when you're actually skiing, you do lose it. By drinking water frequently while on the slopes, you'll maintain your strength much longer.

DESIGNING A DRYLAND TRAINING PROGRAM

The first thing you need to do to begin physical training for skiing is to assess where you are in terms of physical condition. As previously stated, this should be done by a physician if you are 35 or older, or if you have a history of heart problems in your family. Regardless of age, it is most important that you are honest with yourself about what shape you're in. If the most strenuous exercise you've done for the past 10 years is walk from your desk to the water cooler, you are going to have to begin this process slowly. But do start—you'll feel better and ski better if you do.

Keeping a journal of your activities is a great help. Training logs can be purchased commercially, although a spiral notebook will work just fine. Each week, take your weight and record it in the journal, and every time you work out record the date of the exercise session, the primary exercise you did, the duration of the workout, and some brief notes on numbers of repetitions and how you felt. On a daily basis, you should also take your pulse rate immediately upon waking up in the morning, and record this in the diary. Resting pulse is a good barometer of your overall physical condition. If your morning pulse goes up more than 10 beats on a given day, time to take it easy and dress extra warm if you decide to exercise—there is a good chance you are getting sick.

I like training diaries because they help keep me on a consistent exercise program. Once you get one going, you'll find you feel obligated to write some-

9/4 - 4.8 mile run, easy pace
- 50 reg sit ups, 20 "v" situps,
wall sits 30 sec x 3, 20 push ups

9/5 - 18 mile bike
- 50 reg sit ups, 40 pushups, 25 "v" s.u.
- squat walk -- 25 yards.

9/6 - Hunter Creek, 1:25 return.
- rock carry.

9/7 - RAIN !!! - Elementary School Gym.
- 25 min warm up run.
- 75 reg sit ups
- 50 push ups
- 1 min wall sit x 6
- 25 "v" sit ups
- partner carry x 3

9/8 - OFF

9/9 - Hike up shadow MT. (Micke + Tim)
1:50 return.

9/10 - Aspen Club loop -- 1 lap warm up
- stretch
- Ute Trail 18:30 ... very easy.
- 50 reg situps
- 25 "v" situps
- 45 pushups
- 3 min wall sit routine

9/11 - 25 min run
- 50 reg sit ups
- 45 push ups
- 25 "v" situps

9/12 - Mountain bikes up Highlands for 1 hour
- road bikes up Maroon

9/13 - Shadow MT. loop #1, :23
- 75 reg sit ups ... last w/30 sec hoto x 3
- 25 back ups
- 25 side ups (each side)
- 25 outside leg lifts (each leg)
- 10 inside leg lifts (each leg)

9/14 - HARD punch up Ute, then hike along
gentlemens ridge and round about
to Club 1:40 return.

Keeping a training log is helpful for making training consistent and for seeing improvement in your physical condition.

A training partner helps keep you motivated.

thing in it virtually every day. Diaries are a terrific way to monitor the improvement you've made in running various exercise loops you've established around your town, and you'll have a record you can scrutinize to improve your exercise program in the future.

Along with your training log, a great motivational tool is to have a training partner. You can share the experience of getting in shape for skiing together, and knowing that a partner is expecting you to show up keeps you honest about staying with the program. I find it best to work with a person who has similar goals—someone who's getting ready for skiing rather than preparing for the New York Marathon—and who's in similar physical condition.

STRETCHING

All workouts should begin with an easy warm-up period, then stretching. It is important to increase the blood flow to the muscles with light jogging, or easy spinning on the bike, *before* you begin to stretch out. This makes the muscles more elastic and less prone to tearing.

What muscles you stretch, and how, is an important aspect of a conditioning program for skiing. Although you should stretch your entire body, your main area of emphasis should be the legs. Since most of the exercises that follow place demands on the legs, it makes sense that you should have an arsenal of movements to loosen them.

In any sort of stretching regimen, avoid ballistic (bouncing) movements. It is very easy to tear muscles that way, and static stretching—elongating the muscles, backing off slightly, then holding—is much more effective in loosening the muscles up. Always let pain be your guide in how far you stretch. You have to heed the difference between mild discomfort and searing pain when stretching out. Stretching is not a contest.

The following stretching sequence may be helpful if you are not already on some sort of program. In all of these examples, remember to perform the movement until you feel the muscle in question being stretched, then back off a little, and hold for at least 15 seconds.

Toe Reach

Please note that toe reach is not necessarily toe touching. Many people cannot touch their toes, and they should not feel as though they have to force the issue. To do the toe reach, bend over, keeping your back as straight as possible, and

move your hands toward your feet. This movement is designed to loosen up the
hamstring muscles, which are in the backs of your thighs.

Quadriceps Stretch

The muscles in the front of your thighs are particularly important in skiing. Most of these exercises place large demands on the quadriceps muscles, which will inevitably become tight. To loosen them, stand on your left foot, grasp your right instep with your right hand, and gently pull your right foot toward your buttock. Repeat with the opposite leg. You can either balance independently on the foot you're standing on or place one hand against a wall or other solid surface.

Groin Stretch

If you have ever torn a groin muscle, you know it is very painful and takes a long time to heal. These muscles, found on the insides of the upper legs, are responsible for many tasks in skiing.

To do a groin stretch, stand with your feet wide apart—approximately twice the width of your shoulders—place your hands on your left knee, then gradually flex that ankle and knee, allowing all of your weight to come onto your left foot. You will feel a definite stretching sensation along the inside of your right leg. After you've held that position, repeat on the other side.

Calf Stretch

To stretch the calf muscles, stand in front of a supporting surface such as a wall or tree and lean forward until your hands are touching it. Gradually slide one foot back, maintaining a locked (not flexed) knee joint until you feel the muscles in the back of the lower leg being stretched. Repeat on the other leg.

Achilles Tendon Stretch

You can stretch out the achilles tendon, which gets particularly tight from running, by modifying the calf stretch. Lean against the wall in the same way, but instead of keeping your knee locked, flex it at about a 45-degree angle. That will loosen up the tendon, which is attached to the back of your foot.

The achilles tendon stretch and the others that preceded it form a very basic repertoire that should be done, along with others, as a part of your weekly dryland training regimen. For a complete discussion of the subject, read the excellent book *Stretching* by Bob Anderson (New York: Random House, 1980).

Four Basic Stretches

Toe reach

Quadriceps stretch

Groin stretch

Calf stretch
To stretch the Achilles tendon, flex the stretching leg at a 45-degree angle.

OTHER EXERCISE FUNDAMENTALS

After warming up and stretching, you can begin the main exercise segment. That would include either aerobic or anerobic forms of running, biking, hiking, etc., as well as a few ski-specific exercises that are discussed later in this chapter. Once this segment is completed, you need to have an adequate cool-down period. While cooling, you should again stretch and generally allow your body to return to normal operating temperature. It is important not to jump right into a cold shower, as you are often tempted to do, after the main exercise segment. If you do, you may develop severe cramps or your body may go into fatal shock. Showers should be taken in tepid water (more warm than cold) and only well after the cool-down period is completed.

To maintain interest and enthusiasm in your program, you should make an effort to vary it from day to day and week to week. In setting up a weekly schedule, try to work out in different places but still achieve the exercise you're looking for. If your options are limited because, for instance, there's only one loop where you can run, it might help to run the loop in the other direction. You'll be surprised at how different it feels.

Besides adding variety, you should try to split your training days between hard and easy workouts. Hard days are for stressing your muscles so they can get stronger. When you exercise hard, you inevitably feel a bit sore, as some slight tearing of the muscle fibers occurs. Easy days give your body a chance to rebuild itself but still provide an opportunity to improve the aerobic base. Plus, the tightness and pain you might feel after a hard day loosen up with these easy workouts.

Establishing easy and hard workouts is a simple matter of regulating the frequency, intensity, and duration of the exercise. People who are just starting out should probably train only three days each week for 15 to 30 minutes each day, with one medium-hard day in the middle. Each week you should gradually increase the intensity of both hard and easy days and the amount of time spent on exercise. You might even add an additional one or two days of exercise to your week. That may sound like a lot of time to get ready to ski, but to give you a feel for the other end of the spectrum, we can note that a world-class ski racer trains six days a week, for a minimum of two hours each day, with three of those days at very high intensity. For someone with less lofty aspirations, three days each week for 45 minutes each day will get you in excellent condition to ski.

By the way, please don't get the impression that you must train like this even to try skiing. Many people do little or no exercise before coming out to the slopes—and manage just fine. What I'm talking about here is the ideal: what

I wish so many of my students had done before they had come to me in a ski class. Skiers progress faster and enjoy the sport more if, first, they do the right sort of dryland training.

SKI-SPECIFIC EXERCISE

For the best results from physical conditioning for skiing, your training should be as ski-specific as possible. Although you will improve your overall health and well-being with any sort of regular exercise, you can still end up with very sore muscles after a day on the slopes. The main muscle groups you need to train for skiing are in the legs, buttocks, lower back, and abdomen. You also use the muscles in the upper torso and arms to a lesser degree. As you can see, skiing involves all the major muscle groups in the body to some extent. By shaping your ski conditioning program around these muscle groups you can improve your overall coordination and develop movement patterns that will directly apply to skiing when winter comes around. The goal of this section is to provide you with some tips on how to tune your exercise for skiing.

Skiing involves both static and dynamic muscular effort. Static, or isometric-type work, happens when the muscles are held in one position without significant stretching or shortening. An example of that in skiing would be straight running on a smooth slope. Dynamic muscular actions occur when the muscles are extended and contracted. That happens often in skiing—during the light and heavy phases of a turn, for example, or when absorbing variations in terrain.

Many of the following exercises are exclusively dynamic, and others emphasize static muscular work. Try consciously to blend both types into your training program. Since much has been written about most of the following topics, I will not discuss any of them extensively. My intent here is to give you information about the exercises as they relate to ski conditioning and, I hope, to spur your interest.

Running

Running has nearly become our national pastime. Almost anywhere you travel around the country, you see enthusiastic people trotting along the side of the highway. As mentioned, running can be valuable for either aerobic or anerobic training, depending on how hard you do it. Make sure you have a good set of running shoes and are familiar with proper running technique before you embark on this form of exercise. There is a glut of written material on the subject.

Traditional running vs. ski-specific running
Traditional running (left) does improve cardiovascular fitness, but is not ski-specific owing to its straight-line nature. For more ski-specific training, find safe places to make gradual turns while running. Making turns against an embankment (right), for example, involves similar use of muscles used in skiing and also improves coordination and balance.

To get the most out of this exercise for ski preparation, you should find places where it is safe to make gradual turns as you run. Running in a straight line is not a ski-specific exercise, although it will certainly improve your cardiovascular capacity. If you make turns while running, however, you begin to involve some of the specific muscle groups you use when skiing. These muscles —in the back, abdomen, hips, legs, and even feet—help resist the outward forces created by turning.

You can also improve your coordination while running. Cross over an imaginary line with each stride, or run sideways, alternately crossing one leg behind the other. By challenging your body with different movement patterns, you begin to prepare yourself for the new movement patterns you'll use on the slopes.

If your knees hurt from running, don't be a hero. Stop and take the time to find the cause of the problem. A frequent cause of knee pain from running is foot instability. You may need to have orthotics built for your feet by a podiatrist. The purpose of an orthotic is to align the bones in your feet properly, so that they don't roll inward (pronate) or outward (supinate) during your stride. Another frequent cause of knee pain is improper technique when going downhill. Be sure to shorten your stride slightly so that you don't land on a fully extended leg.

Bicycling

Bicycle riding, when done properly, is one of the best exercises you can do for skiing. It is very gentle on the joints and ligaments in the knees and ankles but great for the leg muscles and cardiovascular system. To do it right, you need a bike with multiple gears (either a ten-speed or a mountain bike), and you should select gears that you can "spin." That means being able to keep the pedals revolving at between 80 and 90 revolutions per minute without serious straining. Pushing too big a gear can cause serious problems by damaging the knee ligaments.

There are several other basic rules of bicycling that you should observe. First, automobile drivers tend to ignore you when you are on the road. Make sure you ride defensively and wear a helmet. Toe clips, which are metal or plastic loops attached to the pedals, are also worth spending a few dollars on. They help you get the most out of your bike by allowing you to pull up on the pedals, as well as push down, to generate forward momentum. Also, the pulling-up motion helps condition your legs for skiing (remember unweighting, skating, bump skiing, etc?). Don't be afraid of strapping yourself to the bike with the toe clips. If you don't pull the straps too tight, you'll find you can get out of them easily. Bike shoes, which have cleats to latch onto the pedals, should also be purchased. They're designed to transmit the force generated by your legs to the pedals, making your effort much more efficient.

An important riding technique you should practice is not to ride with locked elbows. Try to keep your arms lightly flexed at all times. This position

A well-equipped cyclist. Note helmet, bicycle gloves, multiple gears, toe clips, and bike shoes.

helps absorb road vibration, but more important, it allows the muscles of the gluteus maximus (buttocks) to be involved in the process of turning the pedals. Since these muscles are very active in skiing, it is important to ride with good form so that you exercise them.

A form of bicycle riding that is particularly good for skiing is mountain biking. Mountain bikes have wide, nubby tires, motorcycle-type handlebars, and 18 gears. They are great fun for riding on fire or work roads and are fine around-town transportation as well. Beyond providing aerobic or anerobic conditioning depending on the intensity with which you ride them, mountain bikes help hone your balance. Since you typically ride on varied terrain strewn with rocks and bumps, you are constantly in the process of readjusting your balance while keeping the bike moving on the hill.

Hiking

Hiking is one of my favorite forms of exercise for skiing. It can supply an excellent aerobic or anerobic workout, and the trails often end with magnificent vistas. Besides trails maintained by the U. S. Forest Service, it's also fun to hike at a ski area. Most areas let you do this and it gives you a chance to check out the true contour of the runs you ski on. You'll find they look much steeper without snow. Watch out for the usual things, such as touching poisonous plants and drinking water from mountain streams (many have high concentrations of giardia, a virus that will absolutely devastate your digestive tract if it

Hiking
As your conditioning improves, try running up short sections on your way uphill. Eventually you might be able to run the entire way.

gets inside you). But also be cautious about going downhill. It's very easy to twist an ankle if you aren't wearing shoes with adequate support or if you step too quickly when unsure of the footing. Also, be careful not to land on a fully extended leg as you move down the mountain. As in regular running, it is much better to land on a slightly flexed leg, so that your muscles, rather than the bone surfaces in the knee joint, absorb the shock.

Swimming

Swimming is not particularly good exercise for skiing. Although you can improve aerobic or anerobic capacity by doing it, you are using muscle groups in the legs that contribute little to skiing. For that reason, swimming should be used only as a general conditioner, or by people who have physical problems that preclude their participation in other forms of exercise.

Boardsailing

Boardsailing is much better exercise for skiing. This sport, which has become quite popular in recent years, helps strengthen the entire body—particularly the arms and legs. Because you have to learn some fairly complex movement patterns to do it, boardsailing promotes general body awareness, which will make skiing easier. Serious demands are placed on your balance mechanisms, and sliding along on a pair of skis seems easy after you've tried to remain upright in a stiff breeze while holding onto the boom of a sailboard.

Martial Arts

Although the martial arts may contribute to a person's overall condition and strength, their primary value as a ski-specific exercise is the mind/body unity they promote. By learning new, controlled movement patterns, a person participating in this sort of training will progress faster on the ski hill. Akido, a defensive rather than an offensive martial art, is particularly good for learning how to move in new ways.

Lateral Hopping

Hopping laterally from foot to foot is one of the traditional exercises prescribed for ski conditioning. It requires a dynamic, explosive use of the muscles in the legs, and it helps reinforce an angular relationship between the legs and upper

A   B

Lateral hopping
As you hop laterally from foot to foot, try to keep your hands slightly forward and out to the sides as you would if you were skiing.

body. To best exercise the muscles used in skiing, you must remember always to spring off a flat foot. Resist the urge to extend with the ankle. You can't do it in skiing since the muscles involved are restricted by the ski boots.

Lateral hops can be done in several different ways, both to promote variety and to involve slightly different muscle groups. You can hop laterally from foot to foot on flat ground, trying gradually to increase the amount of lateral displacement of your body. Or, on a slight incline or in a natural gully, you can hop from foot to foot, allowing yourself to move forward as you do it. Or, you can work on static strength by hopping laterally, then landing and holding your balance for several seconds before you hop back to the other foot. Whichever method you choose, make sure you hop off a flat foot.

Lateral Hill-Bounding

Closely related to lateral hopping is lateral hill-bounding. This exercise, considered extremely anerobic, is an excellent way to work the skiing muscles. Here at the Aspen Ski Club, it is one of our racers' least favorite exercises, but the results are well worth the pain.

To do it, find a moderate incline that's at least 20 feet long. Stand sideways at the bottom of it, lift the uphill foot, then hop laterally up the hill on the downhill leg. As in the regular lateral hop, make sure you extend off a flat foot. After you get to the top, walk back down, turn sideways in the opposite direction, and repeat on the other leg. After that, complete the sequence by lifting the downhill leg and hopping on each uphill foot. Set yourself a goal for how many complete repetitions you'll do.

Backwards Tuck Walk

Although you might not want to do it on the same day, you can use the same gentle incline for walking in a backwards tuck position. This exercise is more physically demanding than the name would indicate. To do it, get down in a low tuck position and walk backwards up the hill. As with lateral hill bounding, set a goal for how many repetitions you'll do on a given day. If the exercise is too easy for you, a variation is to hop up the hill on both legs while in a tuck. This is particularly brutal and, as your legs will tell you, almost instantly anerobic.

Backwards tuck walk
Backwards tuck walking uses almost exactly the same muscles as downhill skiing.

Wall Sits

The wall sit, or phantom chair, is another of the exercises traditionally prescribed for ski conditioning. As you might suspect, this involves holding yourself in a seated position against some flat surface, such as a wall, a tree, or a large rock. The exercise emphasizes the large muscle groups of the upper leg and works them in a static fashion.

To perform a wall sit, place your back against some flat surface, then gradually slide down until your upper leg is parallel to the ground. Don't go down any further, as that will cause serious strain on the knees. This sort of exercise is usually done in repetitions of a set duration. You should probably start out with no more than a 30-second interval and eventually work up to a minute or more in the sitting position. Three repetitions is probably a good starting number. Try not to brace yourself with the hands on the knees, and keep your feet flat on the floor. After each repetition, shake out the legs for at least 15 seconds before starting another.

Wall sit
Wall sits, or phantom chairs, are the best way to develop static muscular strength in the upper legs.

Door Press

Another exercise to develop static leg strength for skiing is the door press. To do one, position yourself facing out in a doorway and lean against one side. Brace one foot flat against the bottom, and press your shoulder and hip against the other side of the doorway. You should imagine that your hip and shoulder are trying to push the wall that the door jamb is attached to. Start out with three repetitions of 15 seconds on each leg, and gradually increase the duration as your strength improves. Like wall sitting, this is a strength-building exercise that you can do regularly at work or at home.

Door press
When doing a door press, be especially conscious of trying to push your entire side—from your hip to your shoulder—against the wall.

Abductor/Adductor Exercise

It is very important to exercise the muscles responsible for moving the leg inwards (adductors) and outwards (abductors). These muscles in the legs are used almost constantly when we make turns but receive little actual conditioning from typical methods of exercise.

Although many health clubs have special machines that can help strengthen these muscles, there are several less expensive ways to condition them. One way is to sit on the ground with your feet flat and have a training partner supply resistance. Have her first hold her hands on the outsides of your knees as you try to pry your legs apart. Next, have her put her hands on the insides of your knees and supply resistance as you try to close them together. Do at least five repetitions each way, then switch places and assist your partner. It is important not to supply too much resistance, as you can easily injury your muscles by straining too hard.

Another way to work the abductor and adductor muscles is to cut up several pieces of an old inner tube and loop them together. Attach them to a tree or a post and stick your leg through the loop at the end. By pulling against the rubber, you can now work your "abs" and "ads" without a partner to supply the resistance.

Dryland Slalom

Dryland slalom is one of the most enjoyable, and potentially most beneficial, exercises for skiing. It involves wearing running shoes and making turns around fixed objects. This exercise is valuable for either aerobic or anerobic training and helps develop a number of skiing skills. Done properly, it teaches you about angulation (keeping your upper body leaning slightly out, rather than into, the turn), upper/lower body independence, timing, making round turns, and many of the other technical components of skiing discussed in the previous chapters.

There are many opportunities for dryland slalom training. Trees, parking meters, or benches on a sidewalk are some of the things I've used to make turns around. You can also use bamboo racing poles if you have them. Serviceable but slightly broken bamboo can usually be found discarded on the sides of race hills at a ski area.

To get the most out of running dryland slalom, there are a number of things you should concentrate on. Learn to make round turns by trying to keep your body traveling in an "S"-shaped line around the gates. To keep from running a "Zorro" ("Z"-shaped) line around the gates, you have to be constantly looking ahead for the next turn.

Dryland slalom
Notice that by leaning out as she makes her turns, the runner angulates her body almost exactly as she would when skiing (see page 64).

After you've learned to do this, try to run with your upper body leaning out, rather than into the turn—in other words, resist the urge to lean the entire body in the direction you're turning. Once you're comfortable with angulating like this, concentrate on having your upper body facing toward the next gate as you finish the turn. This gives you a feel for allowing the feet to turn against the upper body. Finally, by linking all these movements together in a rhythmic fashion, you can begin to hone the timing of your movements, which is so essential in skiing.

Sit-Ups

Sit-ups are necessary in ski conditioning because the abdominal muscles play such a major role in the sport. Since all movements basically originate from our center of mass—located approximately just below the navel—it is important to make this part of your body very strong. These muscles are especially important for making short-radius turns and absorbing terrain variations. Besides the usefulness in training the stomach muscles for skiing, it is well-known that lower-back problems can be prevented by strengthening these muscles.

Sit-ups come in many varieties. Whichever type you choose to do, remember two things:

1) Keep your knees bent. Bent knees are important because they allow you to exercise the abdominals exclusively. If your legs are extended, most of the work will be done by the extensor muscles in the hip and upper thigh.

2) Contrary to popular practice, you should not place your hands behind the head when you're doing sit-ups. This places strain on the neck and may cause serious back problems. Instead, cross your arms over your chest, pressing your left hand against the front of your right shoulder, your right hand just the opposite.

Whether you are doing the classic sit-up (that is, lifting your upper body toward your bent knees), a "V" sit-up (lifting your upper body and legs simultaneously toward each other), or some other sort of stomach torture, make sure you maintain good form during the repetitions. It is very easy to get sloppy and start jerking the body up from horizontal. This results in less effective exercise and may cause muscle tearing. It is far better to do 20 sit-ups well, and rest before doing more, than to flail your way through 50 consecutive bad ones.

Back-Ups

The back muscles get a tremendous workout in the course of a day of skiing. With the exception of lift rides, you are in a standing position the entire time you're on the slopes. Combine this with the demands placed on the back by absorbing terrain variations and you can see how important it is to strengthen this area of your body.

One of the best ways to strengthen the back muscles is to do back-ups. Find a picnic table and lie face down on it with your partner holding the back of your legs. Wiggle forward until your entire upper body is hanging over the end of the table at a 90-degree angle to your legs. Now put your hands behind your head and lift yourself so your body is parallel to the ground—that's one repetition.

As everyone knows, the back is a very delicate part of the body. To prevent injuring yourself while doing back-ups, *don't go beyond horizontal and don't arch your back.* Arching causes severe stress on the vertebrae and may lead to serious problems. To gauge where horizontal is, you can have your partner hold his hand out as a guide for the first few repetitions. It is important to start out with a small number of repetitions so you don't strain the back muscles too much. Ten or 15 back-ups, three times per week, is probably the maximum as you are starting out, and 25 consecutive repetitions is a goal that you should take at least a month to work up to.

Back-ups
Note the position of the body in picture B—only slightly beyond parallel with the ground.

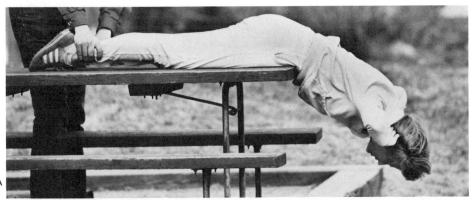

A

B

Push-Ups

Push-ups should be a part of any ski conditioning program. They are effective in developing general conditioning and are particularly useful for strengthening the upper body. You can start your push-ups by having your knees on the ground, but after several weeks you should aim to do them with only your toes touching. For variety and slightly different muscle emphasis, try doing push-ups with the hands at different widths, from very wide to very close together. If you are a true masochist, or a true marine, you can extend your arms rapidly during the push phase and clap your hands at the top of each push.

A

B

A

B

Push-ups
Push-ups can be done at first with the knees on the ground (left)
and then, as you get stronger, with only the toes and hands
touching (above). Remember: Try to keep your back straight during every phase of the exercise.

IMAGING SKILLS

Besides doing ski-specific exercise, the most important thing you can do to improve your skiing when you're not on the snow is to practice imaging skills. When you are viewing and studying correct technique, your mind forms pictures of the movements you want to duplicate on the slopes. This study is beneficial for all levels of skier.

There are many media available with which to look at skiing. Videotape, movies, and photographs all provide opportunities for you to get a picture of the correct movements in skiing. Each has certain strengths and weaknesses, so whichever way you choose, always try to keep what you are viewing in perspective. Snow conditions have a tremendous impact on the technique a skier uses—is he on powder, packed, moguls, or ice? Steepness of terrain is another big factor—the movements a skier uses on steep terrain bear little resemblance to movements used on the flats. Finally, look at the task the skier is performing. A person skis much differently on an easy recreational run than in a downhill race. The key is to look at skiing in context. By doing so, you avoid the pitfall of thinking that you always ski in one particular manner. You don't. Ski conditions, slope steepness, and skier goals are extremely varied, and good skiing involves adapting to the changing demands of the mountain.

Ski movies usually circulate around the country during the fall as a kind of "turn-on" for the coming winter. Since they are commercial ventures designed to entertain their audiences, most ski movies provide little content for serious movement analysis. In spite of this, every skier owes it to himself to see at least one Warren Miller movie in his lifetime. The man virtually invented the genre, and his brand of humor is unique, to say the least.

Looking at skiing photos is a much better option for getting a mental image of the sport. You can find them in all the skiing magazines and in many books. The advantage of skiing photos is that you can easily see what the skier is doing; the tradeoff, of course, is that you only see a brief moment of the skier's turn. Since skiing involves movement, this can be a serious drawback if you don't look at the photo with this in mind. Think, when you look at a picture, about where the skier has come from and what his next movement will be. This is easier when you look at photo assemblies, which are multiple-image photographs. In studying any form of still photography, try to mentally connect the skier's movements.

Videotape has become a popular, and possibly the best, way to get a mental picture of the movements involved in skiing. Unlike movies, videotape offers the advantage of being able to watch skiing at home. You can obtain skiing footage on tape either by recording television ski shows or by purchasing commercially available skiing tapes such as SyberVision. It helps to replay certain sequences or to use slow motion so it's easier to see the movements you are trying to learn. One caution with the use of slow motion: You should always end up watching the tape at regular speed. You're trying to program your brain with correct movements at proper speeds. It is impossible to ski in slow motion.

Beyond slow/fast motion, there are a number of other rules for getting the most from watching videotape. As you watch a skier on video making a turn, try to concentrate on different parts of his body. Rerun the tape as many times as necessary so that you really see what the feet, legs, skis, hands, upper body, and other parts are doing during a given sequence. Then watch the tape at least once to absorb the skier's movements as a whole. Close your eyes and in your mind rerun the skiing you saw, but this time with you in the boots. Now you're on your way to grooving your own muscles to make the same type of turns.

As a sidelight on the topic of video, its usefulness as a tool for on-snow instruction is doubtful. Even though all of us love to see ourselves on television, seeing videotapes of ourselves skiing generally does not enhance performance. What it may do in the mind's eye is reinforce wrong movements. An exception is when a student is positively unable to feel the incorrect movements he or she is making. In other cases, the time involved videotaping a ski class is probably better spent looking at tapes of experienced skiers performing the desired movements correctly.

8

A Few Final Words

Once you've absorbed the information in this book and taken several skiing lessons from certified professional instructors, you're on your way to a lifetime involvement in a good, healthy sport. As I mentioned in the beginning of this book, I can't seem to get enough of skiing, and the more I travel and talk with other skiers, the more I discover that I'm not alone. There are people I know who live in suburbs and cities, who work in offices and factories, whose schedules allow them to ski only a few times each winter, and yet who think about and stay in shape for skiing all year round. You need not restrict yourself to the fall months when following the nutrition and exercise regimen I recommended in the previous chapter. The exercises are a great way to stay in shape throughout the year, and my remarks about nutrition apply even if the next snowfall is a long six months away. The point is that skiing, along with training to ski, makes for a wonderful year-round activity, and if you find yourself getting hooked on it, as I did, there's no reason to forget about the sport when the season's ended. You might, as I suggested earlier, eventually find yourself attending racing camps in southern latitudes, or extending the season by trying summer skiing in such pristine loca-

Helicopter skiing is only one of many adventures that awaits you once you learn to ski well.

tions as Mt. Hood or Mt. Bachelor, Oregon. These North American summer-ski areas afford excellent warm-weather skiing through August, and, if you choose, you can find winter conditions in the southern hemisphere through the middle of September.

Even if you confine your skiing to the normal Thanksgiving-to-Easter season, you'll find that it's great fun to sample as many different kinds of ski areas as you can in a winter, especially if you're just starting out. In the appendix to this book, I discuss the kinds of ski areas available today, with an emphasis on the qualities that make a good one. I suggest that you read that information closely, and remember: No matter who you are or what you want out of skiing, you can always find areas with trails and services specifically tailored to meet your needs.

KIDS AND SKIING

"But I have a couple of kids," you say, "and I'd like to get them skiing, too. How do I go about it?" That's simple. Gone are the days when kids learned from parents sending them repeatedly down a snow-covered slope. Today, most ski areas offer beginner lesson packages for children, and I strongly recommend that a child's introduction to the sport begin there. Enrolling your children in a "kinder school" ensures that they will learn correct basic technique, which will serve as a foundation as they advance in the sport. Also, if you enroll your kids in a group lesson, they will be learning with their peers. Children, like adults, are more relaxed and learn faster when they ski in a peer-group atmosphere, and instructors today have numerous ways to make sure that the lessons remain fun.

By and large, kids pick up basic skiing technique—wedging, wedge turns, christies—more quickly than adults, but a few words of caution here. Kids can be just as petrified of the unknown—in skiing's case, steep slopes, tricky lifts, slippery skis—as adults sometimes are, so go slow with your kids and take the time to introduce them gradually to the sport. You should certainly tell them a little bit about what they can expect when they go for their first lesson. Be present when they meet their instructor and reassure them that you'll be back to pick them up at an agreed-upon hour. Also, make sure your children are properly dressed for the several hours they'll be spending outdoors. This means well-fitting insulated ski boots, parka, and ski pants, a wool hat that covers the ears, and water-resistant mittens. In general, don't just dump your children at their lesson and bolt; skiing is a beautiful family sport, but in the beginning

Skiing classes for children are designed to be instructive but fun.

you've got to work at it with your kids before the beauty shines through. I have friends who say they never feel closer to their kids or have more fun with them than when they're skiing together. The possibilities are there for you and your family. Don't be afraid to start your kids skiing even when they're three or four years old. On the other hand, if they don't want to right away, don't rush them; find the balance. The idea is to keep skiing what it should be: fun.

THE CHALLENGE OF SKIING

Even if you ski a great deal, there can come a time when you feel that you just aren't progressing as a skier, that your skiing's gone stale. When that happens it's time to go to a certified ski school. Enroll in a private lesson, or a mountain experience class, or take a race clinic. Educational experiences like this can work wonders on your skiing: they can help you continue to progress to new levels and reawaken your appetite for skiing's endless possibilities. Every year I encounter people who say to me, in effect, "Yeah, skiing's okay, but it's lost some of its thrill for me." Their problem? They're bored! Why? Because they're not *making the effort* to progress. Usually, I just have to give them a gentle hint to take a lesson or two, and when they do, the old glow is back. They're skiing better, and, more important, become the born-again fanatics they were when they first took up the sport.

As with any activity, to progress in skiing, you not only have to put in the time, you've also got to put in the energy and dedication. There's absolutely no reason—except old age and its concomitant complaints—why you can't be skiing better three or four years from now than you are currently. All it takes is effort. Remember: perfect practice makes perfect. If you want to get better as a skier, you can—if you try.

Of course, once you can ski fluidly on any terrain, the sky's the limit. You have the satisfaction of knowing that you could travel to any ski location in the world, snap on a pair of skis, and negotiate that location's steepest slopes. Sounds like a small satisfaction? Believe me, it's not. Learning to ski well means that through effort and practice and dedication, you've overcome any fears you may have brought to the sport, and nothing stands between you and its challenges and rewards.

To give you a final idea of what those might include, a few summers ago, I stepped into a helicopter with some good friends and we were lifted to a slope close to Coronet Peak, in New Zealand. The day was cold and clear, and snow had fallen the night before, and we touched down to find a virgin snowfield of light, dry powder. The run below us was smooth and sparkling, and we seemed to tingle with anticipation of the perfect snow that beckoned us. We were not disappointed. For the first few minutes, all I registered was the delightful sensation of floating, floating as we carved long "S" turns down the pristine white blanket. But somewhere, maybe after 30 turns or so, I found myself thinking: This is the joy. This is the pleasure. This is what I was born to do.

This sport can stir those feelings in anybody, and the more you ski, the deeper those feelings become. But don't take my word for it, try it yourself. It's a beautiful, healthy addiction.

Appendix: Ski Areas

Ski areas now operate in 40 states, as well as most everywhere else in the world where there are snow-covered mountains. Beyond the places you'd expect, such as Europe, New England, or the Rocky Mountains, ski areas operate in such unlikely places as Georgia, Alabama, Kentucky, and Tennessee. But regardless of where the ski area is located, all have benefitted from technological improvements which provide more consistent, enjoyable skiing.

SNOWMAKING

Making snow is relatively simple, but extremely expensive. The process involves the installation of pipes up the mountain to transport air and water —the raw material of man-made powder. Most areas bury the pipes to prevent the water from freezing, and for safety considerations. Hydrants are installed at various locations along the pipes' length so snow guns can be attached to blow the air and water which is being pushed up the mountain by large compressors stored at the mountain's base. To make snow you simply force the air and water out through the nozzle of the snow gun

183

Snowmaking at many ski areas has progressed to a precise science.

under tremendous pressure. Water molecules are broken up in this process and thrown into the air, freezing into crystals before they land on the slopes. A snowmaking system for a large mountain complex costs many millions of dollars. Although skiing is still dependent on cold weather for its existence, ski areas no longer have to rely on the white stuff falling naturally out of the sky.

SLOPE GROOMING

Whether the snow falls naturally from the sky, or is shot out of snow guns, grooming is necessary to produce a high quality skiing experience. Tremendous gains have been made in this area in recent years. The original grooming equipment, the "Tucker Snowcat," was limited to beginner or low intermediate slopes. Many areas still use these machines as they are extremely reliable and do an excellent job on the terrain they were designed for.

In recent years, however, high powered grooming equipment has been developed. These vehicles, called Hydromasters, Cats, or Pisten Bullys, can travel virtually anywhere on the mountain. They blade down moguls, and pull "power tillers" which leave behind an extremely smooth surface. Today's skier

has come to expect this manicuring of the mountainside. The consistent surface
that good grooming produces has done much to improve snow conditions on
the average day, making skiing much easier—and safer.

NIGHT SKIING

Night skiing has become a typical aspect of operations at day-type ski areas.
As little as 15 years ago skiing at night was absolutely terrible. Incandescent
lights were the popular method of illumination in those years, and the result
was irregular lighting with large shadows dominating the surface. Most lights
of this type have been phased out, and mercury vapor, metal halide, or high
pressure sodium systems are now used to turn night into day.

Thanks to these new methods of ski area lighting, night skiing is very
enjoyable. Besides fitting nicely into the typical work schedule, some people
actually feel that you can see better at night. They say this because artificial
lighting does an excellent job of modeling the contour of the slope. Many people
must agree, since a significant number of all the skiers in this country are
registered at night, and over 50 percent of our ski areas offer this form of skiing.

Be forewarned: You'll usually encounter colder temperatures when night
skiing. But having to put on an extra layer to stay warm is well worth the
tradeoff. Snow conditions are typically better in the evenings thanks to the
cooler temperatures.

For nine-to-fivers, lighted ski areas provide fine skiing opportunities any day—or
night—of the week.

WHERE TO SKI

You don't need a big mountain to learn how to ski. The absolute basic is a snow-covered incline. Besides possibly finding this in your backyard, other likely spots are golf courses or your town's local sledding hill. I am not suggesting that these are the best places to learn to ski, but despite the obvious drawbacks—lack of lifts, instructors, and patrolmen—many lifelong skiers have learned on hills that were painfully small.

The Cochran family from Richmond, Vermont, is a case in point. They have a small hill behind their house, and a number of years ago they cleared the trees and built a small rope tow. Four members of the U.S. Ski Team came off this "mountain," which is less than 100 feet high. All of them became Olympians. Marilyn Cochran won a bronze medal in the 1970 World Championships, and her sister Barbara Ann captured a gold medal in the 1972 Olympics. The Cochrans are living proof that success in skiing is not determined by the size of the mountain you practice on.

Day Areas

Day areas are skiing facilities without an extensive number of overnight accommodations in their immediate vicinity. If you live close to one, you'll find it offers a number of advantages, not the least of which is allowing you to try the sport without having to travel far. Most day areas offer a "beginner's package," as previously discussed, and many offer multi-week, learn-to-ski plans. You might very often find these kinds of packages set up through the business you work for, or a local community group. An example of multi-week packages are those run by the Swain Ski Center, in Swain, New York. This small ski area, about 45 minutes by car from Rochester, offers eight-week-long lift, lesson, and rental packages, costing around $120.00 per person, for businesses and community groups. Their price for school students is even less. Many other day areas also run similar programs. And because of the business schedules of their clientele, most offer these packages in the evenings.

Destination Resorts

As the name implies, destination resorts are places you arrive at, and offer complete services, including lodging, eating, and evening entertainment. Some destination resorts are self-contained communities, such as Copper Mountain, Colorado. At these places you can easily walk around a well-designed recreation village to reach any of its services. More sprawling resorts, such as Aspen or Vail, Colorado, usually have free public transportation systems to shuttle you around during your visit.

You can find out about U.S. and international destination resorts through a travel agent or through advertisements in the skiing magazines. Ski shows, as discussed in Chapter 1, are another method of getting information. Remember: Traveling with a ski club is often the least expensive way to visit a destination resort, thanks to the club's volume purchasing power.

A ski vacation at a destination resort usually covers five days, plus a day of travel on either end. While you're there, consider taking a ski week. Ski weeks are the best way for beginners to get started, and are also excellent for advanced skiers who'd like to polish their skills. Most ski weeks include five days of lift tickets and lessons with the same instructor—rental equipment can be added on if you need it—and evening activities like wine and cheese parties, movies, and a weekend fun race.

DETERMINING SKI CONDITIONS

Drawbacks

Reporting snow conditions remains one of the weak points of the ski industry. It is difficult because a ski report is only a snapshot of a constantly changing situation. That snapshot is usually accurate when taken, but storms may bring powder, rain, changing temperatures, wind, humidity, or sunshine—all of which affect the skiing conditions for better or worse. Since weather changes rapidly—particularly in the mountains—it is difficult to predict how the skiing will actually be when you arrive at the slopes.

Terminology

Although ski areas can't control the weather, they use uniform terminology to describe the consistency of their snowpack and what the average depth of the snow is on the mountain. Most of the words used in ski reports are self explanatory. "Powder," "packed powder," "wet snow," and "icy" mean just what their names imply. Other terminology is less clear. "Granular" refers to snow which has solidified into small, almost circular shapes. "Frozen granular" is often a code word for hard, frozen snow bordering on ice which veteran skiers call "ball bearings." "Spring conditions" or "corn" are similar terms, referring to snow which has melted and was later refrozen by falling temperatures. As mentioned earlier, spring or corn conditions result in icy conditions that are difficult to ski before they thaw slightly, and it helps to wait until mid-morning before going skiing.

Information Sources

You can learn about ski conditions from many sources. Most metropolitan newspapers get information from the wire services or National Weather Service and include this in their sports sections. Personal computers, thanks to data banks such as "The Source" or "Telerate," can provide the same information newspapers use in compiling their daily ski reports.

For extensive reports on current ski conditions, call ski-area, snow-condition "hot lines." Although this usually involves a toll call, it provides the most current information about the area's ski conditions. Ski reports may also be found on radio or television in areas close to ski resorts.

WHEN'S THE BEST TIME OF THE YEAR TO GO SKIING?

The kind of conditions you find at a ski area are largely dependent on the time of the year you travel to the area. Since the advent of snowmaking, many people expect to have skiing at Thanksgiving. While the skiing is often very good at this time of the year, there is no guarantee that it will be. Christmas vacation, besides being one of the most crowded times of the season for a ski area, may also present marginal conditions if the winter is not cooperating. If you are planning to ski during these periods, be sure to check carefully the conditions and the long-range weather forecast.

Ski areas often give their best deals during January. This month is usually a slow one for business, but the snow conditions are very reliable. The only drawback is the potential for big snow storms—typically, it is the coldest month of the winter. With proper clothing, you can enjoy excellent, reasonably-priced skiing during this month.

February is ordinarily the busiest month of the season for a ski area. Many people travel to areas at this time since snow conditions are very reliable, and the presidents' holidays provide vacation time for the entire family. Although the skiing may be very good, be aware that the lift lines and slopes will be most crowded during this month. Less popular areas are your best bet.

Spring is often the best time of the year to ski. It is warmer, sunnier, and less crowded. There is also little chance you'll have to contend with a major storm. These factors make it an especially good time of the year to go to the slopes if you're a beginner. Prices are often reduced in March or April as an incentive to attract skiers who might be starting to think about golf or other recreational activities.

EVALUATING A SKI AREA

Service Industry

However you satisfy your need to ski, you can evaluate an area's performance by the way it treats its guests. Skiing is a service industry. The area is there to provide you with a product, and it depends on you for its existence. If you get the feeling that its management and personnel think it's the other way around (that they're doing you a favor to be in operation), you should go to another resort. Most ski areas treat their guests with respect, but there a few which have forgotten which side the bread is buttered on. Don't patronize the latter.

How to Decipher a Ski Area Brochure

Beyond firsthand evaluation of the resort's attitude towards its skiers, you can learn much about an area by reading its brochures. Although ski-area brochures are naturally written to show an area in its best possible light, there are several things you should look for to determine whether the area is right for you. What is the percentage of "Easiest" (for beginners and novices), "More Difficult" (for intermediates), and "Most Difficult" (for experts) terrain? The National Ski Areas Association has made uniform this terminology, which rates each ski area's terrain in relation to other terrain on its mountain complex. If you are a beginning skier, be wary of ski areas which have high percentages of "Most" or "More Difficult" terrain. Even if you're there for a ski week, you probably will spend most of your time on the "Easiest" runs. If this is only one slope, it will get pretty boring after a while. Also, you won't learn as fast because the terrain that the instructor can select will be quite limited.

Another fact you can learn about from brochures is how much snowmaking the area has. This is very important, especially if you're thinking about purchasing a season's pass or trying to decide on a destination resort for a major ski vacation. If you are making a commitment to use a ski area, you should be certain that they have adequate snowmaking coverage on the runs you'll be skiing. This is less important in places like Utah's Wasatch or California's Sierra Mountains. Ski areas within these mountain ranges typically average over 400 feet of snow each winter. Nonetheless, even where snowfall is almost a certainty, it's nice to have a few slopes where there's some man-made insurance.

If you have a family, another important piece of information you can garner from a brochure is whether the area has facilities for children. Many ski areas offer day care programs for toddlers and a special children's ski school (often called "Kinderski"). You'll want to know if they have these programs, and whether the kids have to be toilet-trained to attend. Children's ski school also starts at varying ages, depending on the area, so you'll want to know about this if you are a parent.

There are a few other things you can learn from a ski-area brochure. How many lifts does the mountain have, and what type are they? Chairlifts are the most prevalent, and provide the opportunity to rest your legs on the ride up. They come in all varieties: singles (the original type, which is nearly nonexistent now because of their low uphill capacity), doubles, triples, and even quad chairlifts. The uphill capacities of these lifts range from around 400 an hour on singles to 1,800 an hour on the quads. T-bars have diminished in popularity in this country, although they are still very prevalent in Europe. These lifts usually get you up the mountain very fast, and since they are less exposed than chair lifts, seldom close down because of high winds. On cold days, gondolas or aerial trams offer the ultimate in protection against the wind. They have totally enclosed cabins, but because of their large surface areas, they will often close down if the wind is blowing really hard. There are also a few poma lifts (sometimes called platter pulls) still around, and these lifts can be excellent, easy-to-ride uphill transportation on flatter beginner slopes. Rope tows, the original ski lifts, are basically nonexistent at this time. If you go to an area that has one, plan on your ski gloves being badly mauled due to the abrasive nature of the rope.

When looking at lift capacities, you should also be aware of where the lifts are situated on the mountain. You can determine this by looking at the trail map. Is there a separate lift for beginners, or, even better, a special beginner section of the mountain? If you're an intermediate and want to try more of the mountain's terrain, find out how many lifts there are that leave the main base area. If there's only one and it's not a high-speed double, triple, or quad, count on long lift lines—especially in the morning on busy days. Lift layout is especially important when deciding on a destination resort where you'll be tied to that mountain's physical set-up for a number of days.

Quantity vs. Quality: Vertical Drop

Mountain statistics are the final factor to consider about a ski area. Vertical rise is the distance from the bottom of the lowest lift to the top of the highest lift on the mountain. The range in vertical drop for ski areas is pretty amazing. Numerous areas have little more than 100 feet of vertical drop and one or two slopes serviced by a single lift. At the other end of the spectrum, there's Jackson Hole in Wyoming's Grand Teton Mountains. Jackson has almost 4,000 vertical feet of skiing, approximately 70 different slopes, and some of the most challenging skiing in the country.

Be sure to keep in mind the reality of the situation when considering vertical drop. If you live in the Midwest or some other part of the country that doesn't have tall mountain ranges, you just won't have large vertical drops. But, as I said in the section "Where to Ski," this really doesn't matter. You can become an expert skier on a very small hill, and the Cochran family from Richmond, Vermont, is a perfect case in point.

What's more important is the quality of a ski area. I have skied many hills which had 400 to 600 vertical feet of skiing, and they were really fun. The slopes had even fall-lines and well-designed traffic patterns. They took pride in the quality of their man-made snow, and their slope grooming was superb. Adequate lift capacity insured minimum lift-waiting time, and the management treated its guests with appreciation and respect. When all these ingredients come together in a small area, you can have a great time "yo-yoing" up and down the slopes.